# Alternative Foods

JAMES SHOLTO DOUGLAS

# Alternative Foods

## A WORLD GUIDE TO
## LESSER-KNOWN EDIBLE PLANTS

'Accuse not Nature, she hath done her part;
Do thou but thine.'
  JOHN MILTON (1608–74) *Paradise Lost*

PELHAM BOOKS
LONDON

*To Desirée*

First published in Great Britain by
PELHAM BOOKS LTD
52 Bedford Square
London WC1B 3EF
1978

Additional illustrations by Debbie Kartum

ISBN 0 7207 0900 8

Filmset and printed in Great Britain by
BAS Printers Ltd, Over Wallop, Stockbridge

# CONTENTS

# LINE ILLUSTRATIONS

# METRIC CONVERSION TABLE

1 inch = 25 millimetres
1 foot = 0·305 metre
1 yard = 0·91 metre
1 square yard = 0·84 square metre
1 acre = 0·405 hectare
1 pint = 0·57 litre
1 ounce = 28·35 grams
1 lb = 0·45 kilograms
1 ton = 1·016 tonnes

# PREFACE

This book has been written in order to provide the average man- or woman-in-the-street, of whatever profession, trade or occupation, with a simple and straightforward guide to alternative and natural sources of food. It aims to identify and describe briefly a wide selection of different edible but lesser-known plants which grow throughout the world under various kinds of conditions. The circumstances of our times, and the constantly increasing pressures and shortages that we have to face, make it vitally necessary that we should all understand how to find and utilize acceptable substitutes for those standard commodities upon which we have hitherto relied for our daily sustenance. Indeed, many ordinary and mass-produced foods are becoming rapidly too expensive, and even at certain periods scarce, for any real dependence to be placed on their permanent and abundant availability. Thus the need for alternative food supplies is urgent and pressing.

Fortunately, there are in existence all around us many thousands of lesser-known but excellent and highly nutritious, though currently neglected, plants capable of providing us with ample stocks of food. It is simply a matter of learning and knowing about them. If we simply sit back and just look to world or national authorities to feed us from the present very limited range of farm and other products, we shall certainly face greater and greater shortages, with rising prices and more suffering. No, rather let it be said now and most emphatically that it is up to every individual to find, grow or collect at least a proportion of his or her foodstuffs, utilizing that vast store of plant material that Nature has supplied in such profusion and prodigality on every side. The same remarks apply equally to families, communities and indeed nations.

It has been stated that the world food crisis is largely an artificial one. To the extent that human beings are at present not making effective use of the full range of the Earth's economic plants, this is certainly very true. The irony is that while millions of people starve or suffer the evils of chronic malnutrition, huge quantities of nourishment almost immediately available from the exploitation and use of the lesser-known food plants are ignored or left to go to waste and never harvested or collected, due chiefly to carelessness, apathy or lack of information and basic knowledge.

Therefore, in offering this book to the public, the author hopes that it will place in the hands of every reader and his or her family or community a tool for tapping some of the enormous store of Nature's food supply that lies now neglected in our neighbourhoods. The lists of lesser-known food plants are international, covering all types of conditions, so that it should be possible to discover within them some products or commodities that will suit every particular circumstance or need, or which may be found, grown or collected, according to the environment in question.

Finally, three things more remain to be said. First, never eat any plant or its produce unless you are quite sure you know exactly what species it is and that it is on the lists of edible material. Second, remember that most plants respond to habitat conditions – you can grow them or collect them at certain seasons, or if you want them out-of-season then you must provide the necessary protection for them. This indeed we do regularly with those tender types that we raise already in our greenhouses in cold areas. Third, with improved communications in our modern world it is much easier to obtain seeds and planting material of new species than it was formerly. If you cannot get or find supplies you want from your local seedsmen or botanic gardens or other sources, you can write to appropriate authorities or merchants in the countries or places where the plants originate and request stocks with a fair chance of success. Virtually all States now have government institutions, botanic gardens, research stations, and private trading organisations which can find and supply seeds or planting material. To import these goods across frontiers, national or international, phytosanitary certificates (plant health documents) may normally be needed and these can be issued by the local authorities. So the situation regarding new seed supplies is not generally a difficult one, if you are really interested.

'Waste not, want not' is the theme of this work. In that spirit let us all go forward and utilize to the best advantage Nature's vast treasure of neglected and lesser-known food plants for the benefit of humanity.

J. Sholto Douglas
Khartoum, Sudan
1975

# Chapter 1

# THE BOUNTY OF NATURE

Nature, in her bounty and abundance, has provided for man's sustenance and support with amazing prodigality. Even a brief survey of some of the many thousands of useful plants that grow and flourish under widely differing conditions and circumstances throughout the various continents of our planet will reveal a substantial proportion of them which bear edible produce or which furnish highly serviceable materials and substances for general consumption. These herbs of the field — known technically as economic plants — have sustained and made possible a succession of civilizations, dating back to the earliest recorded periods of human history. Indeed, without such an infinite range of vegetable life, and the vital ecological balance that stems from it, existence of the kind that we are familiar with today would be impossible.

## Answers to a Question

A very important question therefore arises: why, when there is this remarkable diversity of vegetation and there are such large numbers of plants which can provide food and raw materials for human beings, should there be so much malnutrition and such widespread shortages of essential nourishment in many regions of the world, together with the likelihood of severe famines in the foreseeable future?

The answers are not exactly simple ones, but they can be reduced to one easily identifiable fact — waste. Waste is, indeed, the root cause of all the dreadful and heart-breaking evils of starvation, poverty, insufficiency and food shortage that we see around us at the present time. Because we waste, we want. Nature's bounty is abused and misunderstood. Although we are surrounded by hosts of nutritious plants, we cannot find enough to eat. Modern man has forgotten how to utilize the vast bulk of the vegetable life that thrives so abundantly around him or lacks the ability to exploit it. Only too often he destroys valuable plants instead of employing them to his advantage. Coleridge's Ancient Mariner had some reason when he cried 'Water, water, everywhere nor any drop to drink', for he was bounded on all sides by undrinkable salt water, but twentieth-century human beings, on the contrary, can look out on an infinite variety of edible and nutritious vegetation, ripe, so to speak, for the harvest. Yet this same vegetation, so vital as a source of food, is left generally to go to waste. Here, indeed, is a tragedy — starvation in the midst of plenty.

Waste can be described as a common habit in our world today. Let us consider some aspects of current food production. Of the Earth's total land surface only about eight per cent is well suited, agriculturally and economically, to the profitable and intensive growing of annual food plants, called 'arable cropping', of the types known normally to modern farmers and gardeners. On this comparatively small and restricted area are grown the cereals and vegetables that feed and support the majority of the world's four thousand million inhabitants. The other ninety-two per cent of our continents consists of forests, grasslands and savannahs, deserts, mountains, urban areas and marginal or barren expanses, the greater part of which is little used, wasted or undeveloped. These regions contribute at present only very slightly to human needs.

Twentieth-century farming is extremely restrictive. In the name of agri-business or scientific crop production, modern agriculturists and market gardeners are taught to confine their attention to the raising of a few plant species only and to neglect or discard any others considered superfluous to their operations. Consequently, many hundreds of valuable and potentially important plants are dismissed today in farming circles as 'weeds' or uneconomic types. The general public, in fact, is familiar with a very limited range of crop plants, the products of which are used to prepare the common daily foodstuffs which can be bought in shops.

The progress of industrialization, especially in Western countries – and those other areas which have adopted the Western style of industrial living – has cut off the majority of the population from the land. Crowded into cities and urban districts, dependent upon imported food supplies, and ignorant of the wide range of vegetable foods that their peasant ancestors consumed regularly, these people are compelled out of necessity and by their living conditions to curtail their diets and to eat only those items that they can buy in local town stores and markets. In practical terms, this means that industrial man is restricted to whatever foods farmers and gardeners see fit to supply him with.

From the commercial point of view, it is frequently more profitable, as far as immediate cash returns are concerned, for food producers to concentrate on growing a very few species rather than to cultivate a diversity of crops. The fact that this procedure may well upset the

ecological balance of an environment, damage the health of the land, increase the incidence of plant diseases, and – because of the nature of the techniques employed, which include imbalanced fertilizers and poisonous sprays – create conditions injurious to life in general will count hardly at all where money-making is the sole objective.

The total effect of these different but interlinked circumstances is that today we find that out of the wide range of food plants available to man only perhaps one or two per cent is utilized to any appreciable extent. Our nourishment and standard of life depend mainly on four or five cereals, a dozen or so vegetable and root crops, and sundry incidental species, such as those which provide sugar, oils, fats and similar basic items. Of course, humanity's chief supports are the common grain crops: rice, wheat, maize, sorghum and oats, which furnish essential nutriment for man and his farm livestock. Encouraged by official policy, plant breeders have been engaged for years in hybridizing the popular cereals to secure higher yields. Unfortunately, their efforts have also resulted in the development of varieties of grains which cannot thrive unless supplied with excessive quantities of chemical fertilizers and protected constantly by poisonous sprays or dusts. Should either of these two requirements be absent, the new hybrid varieties may be destroyed rapidly by the attacks of pests and diseases. Moreover, in some cases, the food value of these so-called 'miracle' rices, wheats and maize is notably deficient and the flavour is unacceptable or poor. A similar position exists where numbers of new hybrid vegetable varieties or cultivars are concerned. Tomatoes and other salads especially, as well as potatoes, are now very frequently of low mineral and vitamin content, virtually tasteless, and need much extra care and attention in growing to survive at all in ordinary conditions.

It is clear that the dangers of depending

upon one or two per cent of the world's economic plants, and looking to conventional agricultural and garden practices, as applied today, to supply humanity with adequate quantities of food, are very great. In fact, the position is untenable and the seriousness of the situation demands urgent action. Given the vulnerability of modern hybrid crops, as handled by agri-business interests, a single epidemic of disease in any one year could be sufficient to wipe out the bulk of our sources of nourishment and so cause millions of deaths by starvation. In addition, farm monocultures that exhaust the soil, cropping programmes that upset the ecological balance of whole districts, agricultural systems that break the basic laws of Nature and destroy the health of the land, are consistently and progressively adding to the perils that we face.

Furthermore, because food production today insists on basing its output on such a limited range of crops, it is restricted, as far as arable farming and market gardening are concerned, to a very narrow purview – that of the eight per cent portion of the world's land surface well suited to annual cropping. These are the so-called 'good lands', with the best soils, superior supplies of water and equable climates. The popular plant species and varieties generally used in modern cultivation are incapable of thriving satisfactorily in harsher conditions or on poorer lands. So waste occurs, both of the bulk of the lesser-known, but economically useful, discarded plant species, and of the main mass of the Earth's lands. In short, we have developed a self-defeating system as far as our food production is concerned, neglecting and wasting plants and soils.

## A New Approach

A new approach is therefore needed. Waste of plants and land should be eliminated. By not wasting, we could come to the position of not wanting as far as food is concerned. This new approach is really quite simple and straightforward. In brief, it means the efficient growing and utilization of additional economic plant species. Numerous palatable and nutritious types exist throughout the world, fully capable of bearing good crops of all sorts of vegetables and salads, grains, pulses, fruits and other foodstuffs. Unfortunately, the general public today, as well as the bulk of gardeners and growers, know little or nothing of most of these plants. We are familiar with the common green vegetables, potatoes, root crops such as carrots and parsnips and in tropical areas the ordinary yams and cassava, but of the much greater range of edible species we are largely ignorant. Many of these have superior nutritional content and are of higher food value than ordinary garden vegetables. In addition, they are often far more resistant to diseases and pests, require less care and attention than the generally cultivated types, and can frequently withstand far harsher conditions of soil and climate. Moreover, such lesser-known food plants may demand very little weeding or heavy digging and will generally thrive without special treatments. This ability to grow under more difficult circumstances, in all sorts of places, can be really significant for modern gardeners and householders, who may have few spare moments to devote to intensive cultivation practices and who are concerned mainly with getting good crops of greenstuff with the least possible effort.

There is, therefore, an urgent necessity for all of us to turn our attention towards the lesser-known food plants. Our ancestors and forefathers were not so ignorant as we ourselves are. They ate and utilized Nature's vast store of vegetable provender, often collecting food as it grew wild or encouraging the protection and cultivation of what they regarded as important species. The American

Indians, before the coming of the European settlers, lived well on a rich assortment of food plants found in the forests and glades of the western hemisphere. Today, we throw away these plants or label them as 'weeds' and destroy them wantonly. But the time may yet come when we will be very happy to turn back to such neglected and forgotten sources of foodstuff. Not only can they provide us with vegetables, suitable for inclusion in our daily diet, but they can also give us flour for bread and cakes, porridge, soups and potato substitutes. As the prices of ordinary farm and garden crops rise inexorably, we may be glad to find cheaper and more easily raised alternatives, especially in times of scarcity or need.

## Wide Choice

At this stage, readers who may be unfamiliar with most of the lesser-known food plants may rightly ask: what are these crops which can take the place of, or supplement, the common vegetables generally grown and used at present?

This is a good question and it will be answered fully in this book. Briefly, however, lesser-known food plants can be grouped in the following categories:

(a) Greenstuff
(b) Salads
(c) Beans, grams and pulses
(d) Root and tuberous vegetables
(e) Pumpkins, marrows and gourds
(f) Fruits
(g) Dry grains and seeds
(h) Herbs, condiments and spices
(i) Edible flowers
(j) Water plants
(k) Nuts
(l) Beverages
(m) Fungi and algae
(n) Cereal-substitutes
(o) Fats and oils
(p) Miscellaneous

There are also species that will furnish soap substitutes, medicines and home remedies, materials for domestic use and various other items.

The choice is indeed wide and so many plants exist which are of actual or potential economic value that it would be impossible to include every single type within the scope of this book. In order to avoid confusing and overwhelming readers with such a vast number of plants, care has been taken to present a selection only, which will be most helpful to the average gardener or householder who may be anxious to utilize some of the lesser-known species for food production or for other essential purposes. Because of the importance of the subject today, the choice of plants has been made to include those which may be grown in different climatic conditions or under glass in cold areas. In this way it is hoped that every reader will find something of benefit to his or her circumstances.

## Forgotten Food Plants

In earlier periods of history, many plants that are currently neglected or discarded were regarded as essential items of food. One of the obvious conclusions that may be made with respect to the diet of ancient man is that it cannot have been too bad or poor, for had that been the case human beings would not have survived. We tend nowadays to assume that over the years our pattern of nutrition has improved, that we are enjoying at present a period of life when, for the affluent at least, most food is abundant, hygienic and palatable, and that we are better provided for than our ancestors were. Nevertheless, we are recognizing increasingly our inability to meet the food requirements of the ever-rising world population. In addition, much anxiety is being expressed generally over the high prevalence of nutritionally-related health problems, such as diabetes, obesity, cardiovascular and gastro-intestinal diseases, and cancer, the last named being perhaps the most feared of all. Efforts to overcome these various hazards and dangers have so far ignored the lessons that might be learned from the past relating to our food supplies and food habits and their effects upon our health and wellbeing.

The University of Michigan has for some time been operating a human nutrition programme intended to investigate and examine the history of man's food habits and the resources that have been — and still are — available to him. Research studies have been partly concentrated on the life of the ancient inhabitants of the lower valley of the River Illinois. These peoples existed some five thousand years ago and it has been established that they then consumed a very wide variety of seeds, nuts, berries and roots obtained from hundreds of plant species. Some of these are still growing in the area.

Supporting evidence of prehistoric man's diet is provided by records of the kind of foods that contemporary aborigines eat in Australia, Africa and parts of Asia. These races follow a way of life very similar to that of Stone Age populations. It may be noted that Australian natives enjoy an extraordinarily interesting and nutritious menu, made up of grass seeds, nuts, leaves, berries, shoots, fruits, flowers, barks, roots, bulbs, tubers, saps, resins, insects, rodents, reptiles, game animals, eggs, fish and mosses.

Another people with parallel food habits and diets are the recently-discovered Tasaday in the Philippines.

Now it has to be recognized that aboriginal races, livng in very primitive conditions, suffer high morbidity and mortality from accidents, infections and parasites. Yet it is impossible to deny that most of them have magnificent physiques and obesity, or fatness, does not present any obvious problem in their lives. Even though today we lack any detailed knowledge of the health and food supplies of

ancient man, and no doubt he was affected by periodic shortages and famines, nevertheless the popular image of miserable half-starved cave-dwellers continually struggling for bare survival bears little resemblance to what was the reality.

As far as the variety of his diet was concerned, historically man achieved the pinnacle of success when he was a hunter and food gatherer. But as soon as he began to domesticate wild plants his dietary choices became limited. This fact is very important nutritionally. When human beings started to be more and more dependent on cultivation, their chances of utilizing other food sources diminished greatly. In all those areas where industrial societies replaced the old agricultural communities, a majority of the population was compelled to look to a minority which practised intensive farming. Consequently, we see today that most industrialized countries are forced to rely largely on foods produced from a relatively small number of plant staples, such as the cereal grains and the legumes. The bulk of our foodstuffs, especially in the Western world, are processed in ways that alter their nature and value and which make them differ considerably from the foods of even fifty years ago. Important nutrients are lost in this processing, harmful chemicals are added as preservatives or for colouring purposes, and dietary fibre is frequently eliminated. Modern medical opinion is inclined to the view that these lost food components may be significant in the regulation of carbohydrate and fat metabolism as well as in digestive functions.

The changes that have taken place in industrial man's dietary habits can be related to different kinds of nutritional disease. Originally, human beings were hunters and gatherers, then they moved to subsistence agriculture and finally to dependence on intensive farming. Now, in the life-cycle of man, weaning is a particularly vulnerable time. Breast milk, which is a perfect food for the infant during the first six months of existence, must be supplemented and ultimately replaced by a solid diet that provides not only adequate energy, but also sufficient protein of good quality. When animal protein is short, then a wide variety of vegetable protein is vital. This means eating numerous fruits, vegetables, roots, beans and other commodities. The babies of aboriginal peoples consume such items. The children of subsistence farmers and industrial workers, especially in the underdeveloped countries and in the overcrowded cities and slum areas of the so-called more advanced or affluent lands, do not. On the contrary, they are often expected to survive on cereals and starchy gruels. This serious limitation of diet has just the effects that one would anticipate: energy deficiency due to shortage of protein, in particular kwashiorkor; apathy and malnutrition; and a marked disinclination to develop as normal and healthy children.

Moreover, with the spread of technology, the practice of breast-feeding is diminishing and the use of cow's milk as a substitute for human milk has increased. Lack of money to buy costly tins of commercially produced 'baby milk' and unhygienic habits adversely affect the quantity and quality of this artificial foodstuff, with the result that the disease of marasmus is becoming widespread amongst children nourished in this manner. Intensive and factory-farming methods are responsible for much greater employment of fertilizers, mechanical cultivations, poisons and chemicals, all of which consume energy. Because energy is expensive, the range of crops thus becomes even more restricted. New hybrid varieties of cereals and vegetables, although giving higher overall yields, lack adequate protein values and are deficient in mineral content. Persons eating them therefore do not receive the necessary quantities of nourishment that they obtained from the older strains.

It is not surprising, in view of these facts, that many workers have turned to alternative food resources, in an effort to relieve the world nutritional situation. What are called wild types of seeds may contain considerable quantities of protein, as well as starch, oil and other nutrients, in addition to vitamins. Often, such species have never been selected for domestication, despite their similarity to wheat, maize and commonly eaten grains. With our modern knowledge of plant-breeding techniques and genetics, it would be possible to improve these neglected species. Wild or indigenous plants, native to particular localities, as opposed to exotic or introduced and cultivated types, are often very hardy and adaptable, this being the reason why they are frequently called 'weeds' or why the word 'weed' is attached to or forms a portion of their names. Thus we have pigweed, pondweed and chickweed, to mention only a few kinds. Such plants grow rapidly, thrive easily, and their palatability is well-known in different areas of the world. The application of horticultural and agricultural expertise to their culture and harvesting could do much to utilize this important but forgotten food resource.

Before the introduction of the potato from the Americas into Europe during the sixteenth century, various pulses constituted a large part of the diet of the medieval population. In Greek and Roman times, the plant Jacob's rod (*Asphodelus luteus*), a member of the lily family, was widely grown. The bulbs were eaten in the same way that we consume potatoes today, as a common article of food. The Jewish agricultural tractates of the Mishnah, in Zeraim, give full information about the wide range of food plants cultivated in Palestine. Five kinds of herbs are mentioned which might be used at Passover: field lettuces, peppermint, snakeroot (*Aristolochia* species), wild chicory, and dandelion. The snakeroots referred to here, of different species, grow in Asia Minor and the Middle

1. Chickweed (*Stellaria media*)

2. Milkwort (*Polygala chamaebuxus*)

East; other snakeroots include bistort or *Polygonum bistorta*, a native of Europe, Asia and North America, and milkworts of *Polygala* species, various types of which flourish in Great Britain, the United States, and numerous other countries of the world.

Amaranths, sometimes called pigweeds, have been used since ancient times both for their foliage, eaten as spinach, and for their grains, which can be made into flour for cakes or bread. Many species and types were known to the Aztecs and the Incas, as well as to the early Hindus in India and the Chinese of Confucius' era. Even in Australia, the aborigines ate amaranths as food. *Chenopodium* species, such as fat hen or lamb's quarters, and quinoa, indigenous to South America, are also widespread throughout the world and have been long esteemed for their green leaves and seeds. In pre-Columbian times, quinoa was cultivated in Peru and Chile, providing flour for bread, meal for porridge, and serving as the basis for excellent soup. It is additionally the source of a beverage called *tschitscha*.

Another plant which was formerly much cultivated, but can now be found only listed in gardening books under the heading of unusual vegetables, is skirret or chervin. This produces roots suitable for boiling or for eating in salads. They can also be used after drying as a substitute for coffee. Rampion is seldom seen these days, but was well liked in earlier periods. The plant bears white and fleshy roots, which can be eaten in the same manner as skirret. Hamburg or turnip-rooted parsley grows rather like a parsnip, while the leaves are similar to those of common parsley. It yields large roots, but is not very well-known.

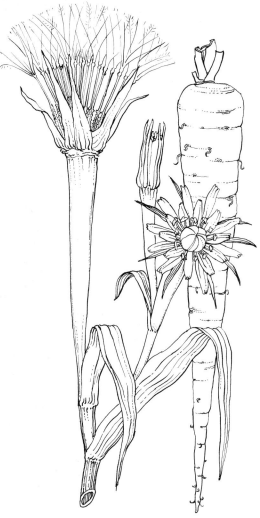

3. Salsify (*Tragopogon porrifolium*)

tasty. In past centuries, the Spanish oyster plant was grown widely, but it is now virtually unrecognized. This species bears good roots suitable for boiling as vegetables. Not dissimilar are salsify and scorzonera, unfortunately little-grown at present, and liquorice root, a Canadian and Alaskan plant, which yields long, sweet roots, often said to resemble sticks of liquorice.

The list of neglected or forgotten food plants can be lengthened almost indefinitely. In going through the chapters of this book, readers may well be surprised to learn how very many useful species and varieties exist.

## Waste and Ignorance

Many gardeners and farmers tend to regard all plants, other than those types that they know, grow and use today, as weeds. In practice, this means that they destroy and exterminate whenever possible all such species. Yet, as our ancestors were aware, large numbers of these so-called weeds are actually valuable crop plants which yield nourishing and palatable foodstuff. What is a weed? It is simply a plant that has got out of place in modern man's scheme of things. We call grass a weed when it grows in our flower beds or in our garden vegetable plots, but when it flourishes vigorously on our lawns we are greatly delighted. Consequently, following this pattern of thought, we are led and conditioned to believe that all plants which are not currently grown on a large or widespread scale are just weeds. This is a very mistaken viewpoint, which has caused enormous waste and suffering.

In the broadest possible sense, we should diversify our gardening and farming, use as many as we can of the lesser-known and neglected food plants to extend and increase our output and so bring vast areas of poorer or wasted land into profitable bearing, to provide ample nourishment for the world's population. This is probably not an idea that can

Few gardeners are aware that common purslane or pursley, also termed the sun plant (*Portulaca oleracea*), is an excellent vegetable. It used to be cultivated extensively in Europe for eating boiled or sometimes raw in salads. Purslane makes good soups. It can be dried and preserved for consumption in winter months. The stems and leaves are very palatable and

be imposed, so to speak, from the top by governments and authorities – it is rather something that should arise naturally and spontaneously amongst the public, starting with individual and, later, group efforts. If everyone of us made a resolve to grow at least a little of his or her own food needs by caring for or cultivating only a few of the lesser-known economic plants, available locally or which could thrive in given circumstances, then a significant and meaningful advance could well be made in tackling the general problem of food shortage. The present national and world systems of food production, by ignoring the majority of useful plants, have tended to weaken and depreciate our stock of nutriment. Beginning with individual or family efforts, drawing on Nature's bountiful supply of health-giving and hardy plants, and using them as domestic and household vegetables, the real possibility exists that a change in attitudes would come about and these valuable species would once again receive the full attention that they merit.

The National Research Council in Washington DC, United States of America, is engaged at present in a study of neglected plants that have promise for aiding economic and social development. Expert opinion has found that many of these species possess exceptional merit, but unfortunately they are still ignored both by commercial farming and horticulture and by amateur gardeners and householders. This is indeed a further confirmation that we are wasting Nature's bounty to our own detriment.

There is an old Scottish proverb that reads: 'Wilful waste makes woeful want.' Although coined in an earlier age this saying has even more force in this present time. Surely, therefore, it is up to all of us to make proper use of all available food supplies and not permit so large a part of them to be discarded and lost by sheer neglect or disinterest.

## A Word of Warning

At this point is is necessary to sound a note of caution. It is simply this: because many readers may be unfamiliar with the appearance of some of the lesser-known food plants, it is never safe to eat any plant that you may see growing, either wild or in gardens and on farms, without first being completely sure that you know exactly what it is. A mistake can often be made and fatal accidents have occurred when people have collected and consumed plants of poisonous types. So take great care to identify plants correctly. If you are not certain what they are, never eat them. Instead take them to some place where they can be examined properly, such as a botanical department, a herbarium or other competent institution. There you will get satisfactory identifications and can then grow or collect the plants of your choice. In former times, when most people were country folk, they knew from childhood what plants they could eat and what they could not; today, the bulk of the population are townspeople and may well be unable to identify edible plants of lesser-known species by sight or from books, so it pays to play safe always.

# Chapter 2

# GREENFOOD FOR HEALTH

Greenfoods, comprising a wide range of palatable and succulent leaves, stems, shoots, stalks and other portions of plants, are considered by many modern dieticians to be perhaps the most important single factor of value in human nutrition. This assessment of greenfoods is based upon two vital points: first, the presence of chlorophyll in the foliage and stems of green or higher plants; and second, the existence of substantial quantities of vitamin C or ascorbic acid – the anti-scurvy vitamin – in the green material of vegetable species.

Chlorophyll is the green colouring matter that we see all around us when we look at ordinary forms of vegetation. It is especially significant for life on Earth because it has the ability to utilize solar energy for the manufacture of starch and sugar in plants. In fact, chlorophyll may be considered as the basis of physical existence. The substance appears to have a particular affinity with the blood, since it promotes the formation of blood cells, normalizes blood pressure, improves the circulation and aids the healing of wounds, according to some authorities. Certain investigators state that vitamin C has been found to maintain youthfulness and retard degenerative diseases. As long ago as 1662, Admiral Hawkins of the English Navy was aware of the value of 'sower oranges and lemmons', which contain substantial amounts of this vitamin, in preventing scurvy amongst sailors who had been a long time at sea and were deprived of fresh greenfoods. Today, we know that vitamin C helps in warding off common colds, influenza and other infections.

## Types of Greenfood

Greenfoods do, of course, include a very large number of different kinds of garden and farm plants. In general terms we can divide green vegetables into two main sections: the cooking types and the salads. However, many serve a dual purpose and may be eaten either cooked or raw. Not only do they possess health-giving properties, but are also normally hardy and grow very quickly in the areas to which they are suited or where favourable conditions can be provided. Many of such lesser-known plants are extremely tasty and can add piquancy and interest to the daily diet.

### SPINACHES

Numerous plants are available which provide excellent substitutes for the garden spinaches. In some cases the leaves may be so tender and palatable that they can be eaten fresh in salads. Here is a selected list of suitable types:

**Goutweed, bishop's or ground elder.** This plant grows to a height of about 2 feet and bears broad leaflets. It is common throughout Europe and the British Isles, as well as in Asia and has been introduced into North America, thriving on waste ground. The leaves are eaten boiled or can be used in soups. Also suitable for salads. Perennial.

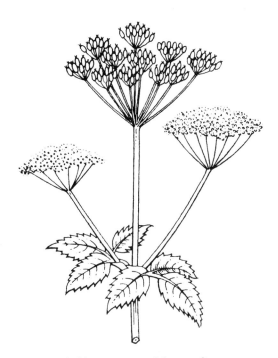

4. Ground elder or goutweed (*Aegopodium podagraria*)

5. Pigweed (*Amaranthus retroflexus*)

**Orange agoseris.** Indigenous to western North America, the orange agoseris bears edible leaves which are eaten in Utah and Nevada. The plant was well known to the local Indians. Perennial.

**Corn cockle.** Grows in Europe and the British Isles and is now common in North America. The young leaves make a good spinach, after boiling, which is sometimes eaten with bacon and vinegar for breakfast. Corn cockle has been recommended as an emergency food during times of want. The plants attain a height of from 2 to 4 feet and bear reddish-purple flowers. The leaves are of narrow shape. The seeds should not be eaten. Annual.

**Redroot, green amaranth, pigweed.** The young leaves and shoots are very tasty. The plant is stout and stands erect, possessing oval-shaped leaves. It is quite widespread throughout the temperate zone and is found in both Great Britain and the United States. In common with the other amaranths it makes an excellent and nourishing spinach, containing notable amounts of iron, calcium, and vitamin A. Annual.

**Prostrate amaranth.** Native to western North America, this plant bears tasty and appetizing leaves, which can be eaten cooked or as a potherb. Perennial.

**Inca wheat, quihuicha.** Very often cultivated, this species is much used in South America, where it is grown quite extensively. The leaves can be boiled, used as a potherb, or eaten in salads. The plant is sometimes called quinoa and was greatly esteemed in the time of the Inca Empire. It should not be confused with *Chenopodium quinoa*, which will be discussed later. Inca wheat prefers elevated tropical areas, but can be grown in the summer in temperate regions. Annual.

**Amaranth or sag.**   A very good spinach, the plants being harvested and cooked when they are at the seedling stage normally. It is much cultivated in India, Africa, China and other warm regions, but will grow in the northern hemisphere in summer time. Perennial.

**Slim amaranth.**   A plant of the temperate zone, used as a green spinach vegetable or as a potherb. Annual.

**Mangostan.** This species is cultivated extensively in Japan, during summer months. The leaves are boiled as spinach or eaten after being salted as a side dish. Annual.

**Mountain spinach, garden orach.**   The leaves make an excellent spinach. The plant is native to Europe and temperate parts of Asia, and has been cultivated. Annual.

**Vine spinach.**   A tropical species, frequently cultivated. The leaves, which may be either green or red, according to the variety, are very tasty. Perennial vine.

**Madeira vine, mignonette.**   Sometimes cultivated, this plant can be found growing from Mexico right along the west of South America to Chile. The leaves are eaten as spinach. Perennial vine.

**Lamb's quarters or fat hen.**   This species has thick leaves which are tooth-shaped and mealy and the stems are sometimes slightly reddish. The leaves and young tops are boiled for spinach. The plants are easily grown and are suited to cold temperate climates. Annual.

**Good King Henry, allgood.**   Named after Henry IV of France (1553–1610), this spinach vegetable grows to a height of from 1 to 1½ feet and bears broader leaves. It is sometimes cultivated. A temperate zone species with high iron value and of good flavour. A much neglected plant which deserves a place in all gardens or household plots. Perennial.

**Quinoa.**   Cultivated since pre-Columbian times in Chile, Peru and neighbouring areas,

6. Lamb's quarters or fat hen (*Chenopodium album*)

quinoa leaves can be used as spinach or incorporated in soups. Annual.

**Ox-eye daisy.**   Common in Europe and temperate Asia and introduced into North America. The young leaves can be boiled as a vegetable and are sometimes consumed in salads. Has been recommended as a famine food in times of emergency. The flowers have yellow disks and white rays. Perennial.

**Winter purslane, spring beauty.**   Originally native to North America, this plant was introduced to Europe. It grows from 3 to 12 inches in height and bears small white flowers. Sometimes cultivated, the leaves and young stems make first-class spinach. Annual.

**Dasheen.**   A tropical species, well-known in hot, moist regions. The young leaves are cooked and eaten as spinach. Perennial.

**Jute.**   The leaves of the species *Corchorus*

7. Jute (*Corchorus olitorius*)

8. Rib grass or ribwort plantain (*Plantago lanceolata*)

*olitorius*, one of the jute-yielding types, make good spinach and are often eaten in West Africa. This plant likes low-lying areas in warm districts. Perennial.

**Canada lettuce.**   Young leaves and stems are cooked. The plant is native to North America and the West Indies. It is considered to be a useful emergency food in times of want. Annual.

**Chinese wolfberry, Duke of Argyll's tea-tree.**   Native to Eastern Asia, but naturalized in the British Isles and other areas. The young and tender leaves can be used as spinach. Shrubby perennial vine.

**Ice plant.**   A plant of the Mediterranean region which also grows in South Africa, the Canary Islands and similar areas. It can succeed in summer in more northern localities. Often cultivated, the leaves being eaten as spinach and in salads. Annual.

**Rib grass, ribwort plantain.**   Grows in Europe and temperate parts of Asia, has been introduced into North America. The young leaves can be cooked as a spinach vegetable. This plant attains a height of from 6 inches to 2 feet. It has been recommended as a greenfood for times of emergency. Perennial.

**Common purslane, pursley.** A low-growing and succulent plant, indigenous to Europe, but naturalized in North America, as well as other regions. Sometimes cultivated and can be eaten boiled, in soups or as a salad. This vegetable can be dried and preserved for winter consumption. Annual.

**Spanish rhubarb dock.**   A perennial African species, grown from Ethiopia to the Congo basin. The leaves are boiled and eaten locally.

9. Garden sorrel (*Rumex acetosa*)

**Garden sorrel.**  Unfortunately rather neglected these days, sorrel thrives in temperate conditions. The tasty leaves can be eaten boiled or mixed with other spinaches. There are various varieties. Perennial.

**Alpine dock, monk's rhubarb.**  Originally a plant of mountainous regions, such as the Balkans, Caucasia and central Europe, this species can be found in most parts of Scotland and northern England. The young leaves are eaten as spinach or in salads. Alpine Dock grows from 9 to 18 inches high and has broad, heart-shaped leaves. Perennial.

**Curled dock.**  A very common species, about 1 to 3 feet high with wavy, narrower leaves. This plant makes good spinach. It is widespread in the temperate zones and has spread as far as New Zealand and Chile. Perennial.

**Patience dock.**  This species attains a height of up to 6 feet. It is sometimes cultivated for its leaves which provide a good spinach vegetable. Grows all over Europe and southern England, as well as western Asia. The taste resembles that of sorrel. Perennial.

**Broad-leaved dock.**  A well-known plant, with broad leaves, attaining a height of up to 3 feet. The young leaves furnish a palatable but slightly bitter spinach. Perennial.

**Mountain sorrel.**  Indigenous to the northwestern parts of North America. The leaves and young stems are eaten in Oregon. Perennial.

**Canaigre.**  This plant grows in the southwest areas of the United States and the neighbouring districts of Mexico. The leaves are cooked as spinach. Perennial.

**Marsh samphire.**  This species thrives in the coastal zones of Europe. The fleshy stems are cooked and consumed as spinach. It is sometimes possible to see marsh samphire produce being sold in the markets of France, Belgium and Holland. Annual to perennial.

**Saltwort.**  The very young, tender shoots can be boiled and eaten. This plant favours sandy, coastal areas. It has been recommended as a stand-by food in emergencies. Annual.

**Garden burnet.**  Common in Europe, temperate Asia, Japan and North America. Garden burnet makes a good spinach vegetable if the tender leaves are picked young in springtime. Otherwise it is good for flavouring salads. Perennial.

**Dandelion.**  Improved large-leaved varieties are available, although the plant is found growing naturally in great numbers. The leaves make good spinach after cooking quickly. Perennial.

**Bigstring or stinging nettle.**  The young tops of stems and leaves when boiled are eaten as spinach or used in soups. A useful emergency food plant. Perennial.

10. Bigstring or stinging nettle (*Vortica dioica*)

11. Dog or small nettle (*Vortica ureus*)

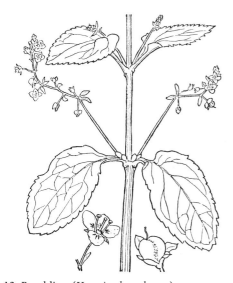

12. Brooklime (*Veronica beccabunga*)

**Dog or small nettle.** This can be used in the same manner as the bigstring nettle. Annual.

**Brooklime.** Often seen in Europe, temperate parts of Asia, Japan and other areas. It likes damp localities. The leaves and stems make a palatable spinach. Perennial.

**Belembe.** A native of tropical America, cultivated in the West Indies. The young unfolded leaves are used as spinach, or in stews and soups. Perennial.

**Caracu.** Grows in the same areas as Belembe, and is eaten in a similar manner. Perennial.

**Yellow yautia, yautia amarilla, tanias.** Another tropical American species. The young leaves are boiled and consumed as spinach. Perennial.

**Primrose malanga, Indian kale.** Similar to the above three species of plants. The young leaves can be chopped up and boiled as spinach. Perennial.

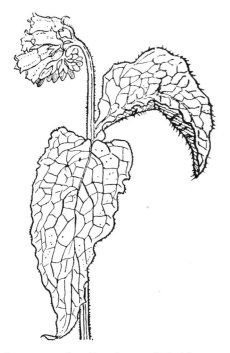

13. Common comfrey (*Symphytum officinale*)

**Common comfrey.** A European species, which has been introduced into North America. The plant grows about 2 to 3 feet high and provides leaves and young shoots which make very good spinach. It likes fairly moist conditions. A valuable emergency food. Perennial.

**Sweet potato leaves.** These can be picked continuously as the plants grow, leaving just enough to enable normal development to proceed. The foliage makes a tasty and nourishing spinach. There are a number of cultivated types readily available.

**Country spinach.** This comes from a plant suited to warm areas called *Basella alba*. It is similar to vine spinach. Perennial.

**Ulluco.** The leaves of this plant, indigenous to Peru and Bolivia, as well as Colombia, but introduced in other countries, make first-class spinach. Perennial.

## BRASSICA GREENS

Our common cabbages and cauliflowers belong to the Brassica species, but there are also many other types of this family which yield valuable greenfood, although they are little-known to gardeners and householders. These species are noted for their calcium and iron content. Here are a few selected kinds that are not difficult to grow:

**Japanese mustard.** This plant is cultivated in Japan, where the soft, thin leaves are gathered and cooked to produce a good green vegetable. Annual to perennial.

**India mustard.** The leaves are eaten after cooking. There are several attractive varieties. Common in Asia and Europe. Annual to perennial.

**Rape, colza.** The seeds on germination will produce succulent green shoots and small leaves which should be eaten before they grow too large. It is at this stage that they are in their most palatable condition for household consumption. Annual.

**Pak-choi, Chinese cabbage.** Resembles Swiss chard in appearance and may be eaten cooked. There are many varieties for garden use. Annual.

**Pe-tsai, Chinese cabbage.** This plant looks somewhat like cos lettuce, but is used normally as a cooked vegetable. Annual to biennial.

## SALADS

**Seabeach sandwort.** A native of northern temperate and arctic regions, this plant is suitable for eating as a fresh salad. The leaves can also be soured or consumed with a light dressing of oil. Perennial.

**Puget balsamroot.** Common in western North America, the young sprouts are eaten raw, especially in British Columbia, Oregon and Washington, Perennial.

**Scurvy grass.** Also called winter cress, this species is indigenous to western Europe, but has become naturalized in North America. It is

14. Ox-eye daisy (*Chrysanthemum leucanthemum*)

sometimes cultivated as a winter salad. Biennial.

**Yellow rocket.**    This is another temperate-zone plant, occasionally used in salads. It belongs to the same family as scurvy grass. Biennial or perennial.

**Saltwort.**    This small shrub grows in the West Indies, Florida, Mexico and Hawaii, amongst other places. The leaves are slightly salty and add flavour to salads. Perennial.

**American sea rocket.**    A North American species, found along beaches and sea shores. The leaves are consumed in salads. It is recommended as a useful stand-by in times of scarcity. Perennial.

**Ox-eye daisy.**    Another plant of value in periods of food shortage, the ox-eye daisy furnishes palatable leaves for salads. It is a native of temperate Europe and Asia, but has been introduced into North America. Perennial.

**Samphire.**    The leaves have a salty taste and add piquancy to salads. It belongs to temperate areas. Perennial.

**Sea milkwort.**    Common in Europe and temperate Asia and has also been introduced into North America. The young shoots are eaten in salads. This plant has been recommended as a useful food in times of emergency. Perennial.

**Waterleaf.**    This plant grows in eastern and southern parts of the United States. The young shoots may be eaten in salads. It was much used by the early settlers. Perennial.

**Cat's ear.**    Found in Europe and Siberia, a valuable food in times of shortage. The young leaves make excellent salads. Perennial.

**Canada lettuce.**    Although mainly used as a spinach substitute and potherb, Canada lettuce leaves, when very small, add taste to salads. A native of North America. Annual.

**Perennial lettuce.**    The young or blanched leaves make good salads. Indigenous to central and southern Europe. It can also be grown in northern latitudes outside in summer. Perennial.

**Ice plant.**    Found in southern Africa, the Canary Islands, and the Mediterranean area. It can be cultivated out-of-doors during summertime in colder regions. The leaves are used in salads. Annual.

**Nasturtium.**    Grown in southern Europe, the *Nasturtium palustre* is a different plant from the ordinary water cress (*Nasturtium officinales*), but is used in similar manner for salads. Perennial.

**Montia.**    Eaten in salads, especially in parts of France. A native of southern and central Europe. Perennial.

**Large evening primrose** (*illustrated overleaf*).    The young shoots are tasty in salads. Found in Europe and North America. Biennial.

**Dotted saxifrage.**    Indigenous to western North America. The leaves are succulent and may be eaten raw in salads or dressed with oil. Perennial.

**Mountain lettuce, deer tongue.**    Used in

15. Large evening primrose (*Oenothera biennis*)

16. Kerguelen cabbage (*Pringlea antiscorbutica*)

salads, especially in the mountains of southern Pennsylvania. Native to eastern United States. Perennial.

**Venus' comb.**   This plant is also called Landy's comb and may be found in temperate Europe. It has been acclimatized in North America. The young stem tops are eaten in salads. Annual.

**Grand comb.**   Common in Greece and Asia Minor, this plant is much esteemed as a salad. Perennial.

**Garden burnet.**   The young leaves are eaten in salads, imparting a characteristic flavour to the dish. The plant is found in Europe, North America and Japan, as well as temperate Asia. Perennial.

**Kerguelen cabbage.**   An Antarctic species, this plant provides good leaves for salads. It is noted for its vitamin C content. Perennial.

**Common purslane, pursley.**   Cultivated in some countries. It can be eaten in salads. The plant is succulent and has a low habit. Native

to Europe, but introduced into North America. It can be preserved for winter consumption. Annual.

**Crowfoot plantain, buckshorn plantain.**   The leaves may be consumed in salads. The species is found in Europe, Asia and North Africa, and has been acclimatized in Australia and New Zealand. Annual.

**White stonecrop, wall pepper.**   May be seen growing in Europe, temperate parts of Asia and North Africa. It is used in salads. Perennial.

**Jenny stonecrop.**   The succulent leaves are eaten in salads. Perennial.

**Rose-root.**   Found in Europe and North America. The leaves are eaten fresh or may be salted. They are also excellent when dressed with oil. The plant is a succulent, with a low habit. Perennial.

**Holy thistle.**   Found in the Mediterranean region, sometimes under cultivation, this species has an ornamental value. The very

17. Dandelion (*Taraxacum officinale*)

18. Sharp-leaved asparagus (*Asparagus acutifolia*)

young leaves are suitable for salads. Annual to perennial.

**Para cress.**   A warm-region species, widely distributed. The leaves can be used in salads. Perennial.

**Dandelion.**   Widely found in temperate areas. Dandelions make excellent and nutritious salads. The leaves may be eaten green or blanched. There are a number of improved large-leaved varieties, such as 'Coeur Plein', 'Ameliore Géant', and 'Vert de Montmagny'.

**Shore podgrass.**   A useful emergency food plant, the very young leaves being suitable for consumption in salads. Native to northern temperate zone. Perennial.

**Common nasturtium.**   The young leaves have a distinctive taste and can be enjoyed mixed into salads. Perennial.

**Edible tulip.**   The leaves make a good green addition to salads. Indigenous to China and Japan. Perennial.

**Italian corn salad.**   Native of the Mediter-

ranean region, often cultivated. The leaves make an excellent salad. Annual.

**Corn Salad.**   Found in Europe, North Africa and the Caucasus, and introduced into North America, this plant is much liked in salads. Improved strains exist for household use. Annual.

### ASPARAGUS SUBSTITUTES

**White asparagus.**   Sold as *asperge sauvage* in the markets of Algeria, being collected on the high North African plateaux. The young stems are similar to those of the garden species. Perennial.

**Shiny asparagus.**   Native of China and Japan, this plant produces tubers which taste like ordinary asparagus. They can be boiled as vegetables or preserved with sugar. Perennial.

**Sharp-leaved asparagus.**   A Mediterranean plant, grown from Spain to Greece and also in the Near and Middle East. The stems are eaten as an asparagus vegetable. Perennial.

**Abyssinian asparagus.** Found in Eritrea and Ethiopia, this species produces stems and roots that can be fried and eaten as a vegetable. Perennial.

**Hathawariya.** Common in Sri Lanka (Ceylon) and eastern India. The plant bears stems and fleshy roots of edible quality. Sometimes the roots are candied and eaten as a sweetmeat. Perennial.

**Seminole asparagus.** Found in Florida and Georgia. Young shoots eaten as asparagus. Perennial.

**Tepejilote.** This is a small Mexican palm, the spathes of which, when unopened, are eaten as asparagus. The plant requires protection from cold in northern climates, being grown as a hothouse species.

**Cistanche.** A parasitic plant, native to North Africa. The stems and shoots make a good asparagus substitute. Perennial.

**Asparagus bush.** The young shoots of this woody plant are consumed as asparagus in tropical Africa. Perennial.

**Sea holly.** Found along the Mediterranean, Atlantic and North Sea coasts. Bears spiny bluish-green leaves with white edges and veins and has a creeping habit. The very young tops of the roots are consumed as asparagus. Height about 6 to 12 inches. Perennial.

**Common pokeberry.** A North American plant, the young shoots of which make a good substitute for asparagus. Perennial.

**Bellwort.** Another North American plant, found in the eastern states, which bears tasty shoots. When young these make a palatable asparagus. A valuable emergency food species. Perennial.

**Common comfrey.** The shoots of this species can be used as an asparagus substitute.

### ALTERNATIVES TO CELERY

**Archangelica.** A plant of northern latitudes, found in North America, especially Alaska, and north-east Asia. It is slightly aromatic and makes as good substitute for celery. Perennial.

**Garden lovage, bladder seed, lovage angelica.** When the leaves are blanched they resemble celery, with a pleasant flavour. Perennial.

**Lesser celandine.** Indigenous to Europe and temperate Asia, with long-stalked, heart-shaped leaves, which when blanched, can be used as a substitute for celery. Perennial.

**Maceron, Alexanders.** Formerly much grown and used. It is a Mediterranean species, extending to the Caucasus and the Canary Islands, as well as Syria. Gradually displaced by celery and so became neglected. A valuable plant, which should be reintroduced into the list of vegetables. It grows wild in the British Isles. This species attains a height of from 2 to 4 feet. Biennial.

**Sweet cicely.** The crisp stalks make a good celery substitute after light cooking.

### OTHER GREEN VEGETABLES

**Thistles.** These are *Cirsium* species, spiny and prickly, but of good food value when cooked. Various parts of the plants are useful for different culinary purposes. Drummond's thistle bears roots which are eaten in the north-western areas of the United States. It is perennial. Another edible species is the Cheyenne thistle, the soft, sweet stems of which, when peeled, form a palatable dish. This is also a North American type. The cooked roots of the wobbly thistle, as well as related species such as the western thistle, the Virginia thistle and the Scopoli thistle, are consumed as vegetables. They can also be dried and stored for winter usage. All these plants have been recommended as reserves for times of food emergency. The foliage and succulent stems of the Siberian thistle, when young, are consumed as greenfood. The tuberous thistle, a European species, with large, spindle-shaped roots, can be harvested in autumn, and if desired, the tubers stored for

19. Lovage (*Levisticum officinale*)

20. Creeping or Canada thistle (*Cirsium arvense*)

eating during the cold weather. This is another plant that has been suggested as a good crop for periods of shortage. The roots are palatable and well-flavoured. The creeping thistle, also called the Canada thistle, is common in temperate Europe and Asia and has been introduced into North America. This plant has the useful property of being able to coagulate milk to make various household dishes.

**Udo.** This perennial plant is cultivated in Japan, the stalks and soft stems being eaten as greenfood. There are several horticultural varieties. The leaves are large and pinnate and the species grows to a height of 5 to 6 feet. To improve the taste and appearance of this vegetable, blanching of the stalks is often practised. Very similar to udo is Chinese aralia, the young leaves of which make an excellent vegetable.

**Orange flame flower.** A native of the south-western United States which bears roots of good quality. These may be cooked as a vegetable. Perennial. Potherb flame flower belongs to the same family and carries the alternative name of surinam purslane. It tastes of purslane and can be used in a similar manner in menus.

**Chayote, chocho, guisquil.** This is a native of central America, but grows in the southern United States. The fruits and young shoots are consumed as a vegetable, while the roots are also edible. There are several varieties of economic value. The plant is a perennial robust creeper, with leaves rather like those of a cucumber. It is propagated by inserting the entire one-seeded fruit into a mound of well-manured soil. The vines require supports and will commence to bear three to four months after sowing. The fruits, used as vegetables, weigh from 2–3 lbs each and are pale green or white in colour and up to 6 inches in length with wrinkled surfaces or skins.

**Great scandix, grand comb.** The young plants can be boiled or fried for culinary purposes. Common in Greece and Asia Minor. Allied to this species is Venus' or Landy's comb, also called shepherd's needle, found in England and North America, which provides tender green tops for consumption. Grand comb is a perennial, but shepherd's needle is an annual species.

**Canaigre.** This plant is native to the south-western United States. The leaf stalks may be boiled and used in pies, while the leaves make good greens for general meals. Perennial.

**Common purslane.** Apart from its use in salads, purslane can be eaten as a cooked vegetable. It also makes excellent soups, because the leaves and stems are very palatable. The plants may be preserved for winter consumption.

**Comfreys.** There are several species, including the common, prickly, blue, oriental, caucasian, tuberous, great and large-flowered comfrey. The young foliage of these plants resembles spinach, while some have edible roots and stems.

## Culture of Greenfood

Plants and crops grown for leaf production require above all plentiful supply of nitrogen. This element fosters luxurious development and gives good big foliage spreads, which are what the gardener, farmer or householder wants in greenfood. In horticultural terms, we call leaf and stalk vegetables 'gross feeders', so liberal manuring is essential if maximum yields and production are to be achieved. Farmyard manure, compost, organic substances and residues of different types and similar materials, supplemented as necessary by nitrogenous fertilizers, make for excellent responses by the plants. Water, too, is important, because the large leafy area demands ample moisture. At the same time, waterlogging is detrimental and care should be taken to ensure that effective and efficient drainage systems operate to prevent excessive accumulation of ground water. In hot and dry summers, irrigation may be needed.

Depending on the plants grown, seeds can be sown in beds, pots or boxes and later transplanted. Alternatively, they may be spread in drills or broadcast and the young seedlings thinned out or culled as they develop to give adequate spacing. Weeding between rows is helpful, since if this is not done periodically, other plants may choke the greenfood crops and deprive them of moisture and nutrients obtained from the soil.

Greenfood crops should take their place in a rotation with leguminous or pulse plants, potatoes or other roots (for land cleaning) and cereals. They may also be intercropped very profitably. To save time when gathering plants from natural country surroundings, local guide-books to wild species should be consulted beforehand to find out the areas in which different types occur most frequently.

In gardening practice, lesser-known green vegetables can be grouped according to type. Thus, when we are producing spinach substitutes we should give them treatment similar to ordinary spinaches – that is to say, care for them in a way resembling that which we would use if we were growing the common, well-known kinds. The same procedure also applies to cabbage or brussels sprouts types and to other groups of food plants. It is quite simple to put any plant listed in this book into its class and category by reading the description given after its name, noting the purpose for which it is employed and observing the culinary uses to which it may be put. Some practical guidelines to growing lesser-known greenfoods are given below.

### SPINACH TYPES

These plants are generally quick-growing and

can utilize plenty of manure and compost. They will benefit from periodic dressings of a nitrogen fertilizer, such as ammonium sulphate. Adequate watering is essential, because the large leaf-area can soon wilt and dry up if moisture is insufficient. It is usually necessary to thin out seedlings when they are a few inches high to give more space for good development. Climbing spinach types can be supported on sticks, wires or strings.

BRASSICA GREENS

The main concern here is to ensure that the crop receives enough water without causing a lack of root seration. Waterlogging affects the plants seriously and soon leads to bad growth or death. Brassica types use a lot of nitrogen. In addition, phosphate is highly beneficial, together with some iron. Fortnightly applications of ammonium sulphate and superphosphate, at the rate of about one ounce per square yard, will encourage good leafy development. To each pound of the main fertilizers, enough iron sulphate to cover the nail of your little finger can be added. Care should be taken to mix this well in with the ammonium sulphate or the superphosphate, to obtain even distribution. It is very important when cultivating brassica greens to see that there is no temporary check to growth, since that will prevent good development and produce stunted vegetables.

SALADS

Because they are normally eaten raw, salad crops should mature with delicate and pleasant-tasting foliage and stems. Bitter or tough leaves will make salads unpalatable and spoil their flavour. Consequently, every effort should be made to give plants intended for eating in salads suitable shade in hot areas and protection from wind and heavy rain in cold districts. Careful handling during planting out is vital, because damaged seedlings will produce badly shaped or malformed leaves.

Excessive moisture around the stems or lower foliage will result in rotting or mildew. At the same time, salads should never be allowed to become too dry whilst growing, or wilting will occur with permanent damage to the delicate leaves. To obtain fine-tasting and blanched foliage, the outer leaves of many salad plants can be drawn together and tied up, to exclude light from the heart of the plant. Alternatively, if they are of small and compact type, the plants can be covered with inverted flower pots or boxes, adjusted so that some air goes through the bottom, but scarcely any light. This blanching process normally takes about ten days and should only be done shortly before the crop is mature or growth and succulence will be diminished.

ASPARAGUS SUBSTITUTES

The thickened stems or other plant parts form the asparagus-type vegetable product that is so much esteemed in menus. These species are generally gross feeders and need large amounts of potash and phosphates as plant food. Sulphate of potash and superphosphate fertilizers can be added to the beds periodically. Wood ashes and salt are also good top-dressings. The soil should be of moderate or faily loose texture, with no waterlogging and plenty of aeration. To secure white or light-coloured produce, the plant parts that are to be eaten can be covered with celluloid or non-translucent plastic material. This will induce blanching.

ALTERNATIVES FOR CELERY

These plants thrive and yield good produce when given a reasonable amount of shade. If too exposed they will produce tough vegetables. Blanching may be practised to secure a good colour. To obtain succulent celery substitutes, plenty of nitrogen, either as manures or with a supplement of ammonium sulphate – or better still, sodium nitrate – is desirable. Waterlogging is objectionable and roots should be well aerated, to avoid rotting.

## OTHER VEGETABLES

Edible thistles are often found in grassy and waste localities, frequently on chalky land. Plants such as udo and chayote need richer soils, with ample manuring. Purslane generally likes more acid kinds of soils, whilst the comfreys have rather variable preferences; common comfrey thrives on damper ground, turberous comfrey does best in shady spots, and the Russian, prickly and soft comfreys are most suited to drier places.

## Cooking

To secure the best results in cooking greenfoods, the following hints should be of aid:

(a) Try to choose vegetables of approximately the same size or else cut up the plant material into even-sized pieces
(b) Never cook vegetables for too long in water
(c) Avoid inspidly-flavoured greenfood by using proper seasoning. Vegetables should be sprinkled with a little salt during cooking and when done should be tasted and reseasoned if necessary
(d) Use the liquid in which vegetables have been cooked as an ingredient of any sauce you may make to go with them
(e) Serve vegetables as quickly as possible after cooking or the flavour may be spoilt or lost

Green vegetables provide vitamins, C, A and $B_1$ as well as calcium, phosphorus, iron, carbohydrate, roughage, and some protein. It must be remembered that as soon as greenfood is cut or pulled from the ground it begins to lose vitamin C. Hence the great importance of trying to grow or collect your own vegetables and eat them the same day, because as much as forty per cent of the vitamin C content may be lost within twenty-four hours after harvesting. Shop and store-bought vegetables are stale and provide very little ascorbic acid to the consumer.

The vitamin C content of greenfood is also destroyed by bad cooking. Even with good and conservative culinary methods, some of the value will be dissipated. Consequently, whenever possible, try to eat your green leaves and stalks or other produce fresh, in salads. Soaking for a long time in water before cooking is undesirable, too, and bicarbonate of soda should never be put in the cooking water: both practices spoil the flavour and texture of the greenfood and destroy both vitamin C and vitamin $B_1$ or thiamine content. Grating or shredding of vegetables is wrong, since these again cause heavy loss of vitamin C. The only way to check this loss is to place the vegetables immediately after shredding or grating in boiling water, but then some damage is still inevitable in the cooking process itself. Remember that the darker outer leaves of green plants contain more vitamin A than do the inner, paler leaves, so do not discard them, but use them carefully.

There are hundreds of different ways of cooking greenfood, both for a mixed and vegetarian diets, details of which will be found in reputable cookery books, but the points mentioned above will serve to provide general guidance for improving results and maintaining the nutritional value of your vegetables.

## PRESSURE COOKING

Cooking by this method cuts down the time spent in preparing vegetables for the table. A good rule is to cook at 15 lbs pressure and time accurately. Use half a pint of water for most vegetables and sprinkle them with salt – do not just put it in the cooking water. Bring them quickly to the required pressure and reduce this rapidly when they are done. Most greens take from three to six minutes, while stalks can need up to seven minutes, depending on their solidity.

## Preserving

This can be carried out in various ways: by drying or dehydration, by canning and bottl-

GREENFOOD FOR HEALTH    37

ing, or by freezing. Sun-drying is practicable in warm countries, but in cold and damp lands it is more costly and difficult. Use must then be made of the few sunny days available and recourse had to the kitchen oven or the airing cupboards. Home bottling is not much of a problem, while for canning quite convenient outfits may be bought for household purposes. Freezing is probably the simplest method for general use. Green vegetables can be quick-frozen for later consumption. By collecting, buying or harvesting produce when it is most abundant, money can be saved, since the preserved food can last for many months. It is important to bear in mind that all your vegetables can be kept in a freezer. After collection, they must be cleaned and packed with a minimum of delay, so that no freshness is lost and the full benefits of the process will be secured.

# Chapter 3

# ENERGY PROVIDERS

A large part of our daily diet is made up of carbohydrates – starchy and sweet foods – which are the fuel, so to speak, on which our bodies run and which provide much of the energy that we require. Roots and tubers, corms, bulbs and rhizomes, as well as rootstocks and other underground portions of plants, are the natural raw materials that we eat, plus cereals, to give us vital carbohydrates. These items constitute a very important section of field produce. We have only to think of potatoes, turnips, parsnips and carrots, together with the flour that we consume in bread and cakes or porridge, to realize how significant these substances are in our lives. As well as starches and sugars, healthy existence demands an intake of fats and proteins, together with necessary vitamins and minerals. Roots and tubers can supply appreciable quantities of these last two items and also some protein, but do not generally contain much fat.

Large or fleshy subterranean portions of plants are actually reserve food stores. Roots and tubers are mostly developed by perennial or biennial plants, though in practice many of these species are treated and grown as annuals. This is because, in nature, they spend the first season of growth in developing the root, tuber, bulb or rhizome, whose store of nutriment they would normally draw upon or exhaust during the following season or seasons in producing stems, flowers and seeds. When we harvest or collect plants with big roots or

tubers, we are benefitting from the stored foodstuffs contained in them.

## Types of Lesser-known Roots and Tubers

There are many hundreds of palatable and nutritious species of plants bearing good yields of roots, tubers, bulbs, corms and rhizomes. Unfortunately, the general public today, as well as the bulk of gardeners and farmers, know little or nothing of most of these types. We are familiar with the common potatoes, beets, turnips and parsnips, which may be seen in any vegetable plot, and in tropical areas with yams, cassava, and a few more species, but the vast majority of root-yielding plants, which our ancestors knew and utilized to full advantage, are now virtually lost to sight.

Let us now therefore consider some of the various kinds of little-known or neglected plants which can furnish us with nourishing and succulent roots, tubers, rhizomes or bulbs for daily consumption. You can think of almost any common garden vegetable within this category and you may be fairly sure to find an acceptable substitute, either growing wild or seldom cultivated. Garden and farm plants are so subject to disease and need such a lot of protection in the form of pesticides and poisonous chemicals, that it is something of a relief to turn towards other species that may better withstand natural conditions and may

21. Asphodel (*Asphodelus luteus*)

not require a great amount of continuous and expensive care.

### SUBSTITUTES FOR POTATOES

Potatoes are a staple foodstuff and it is important to know what we could do if supplies became unavailable or too costly or were suddenly wiped out by epidemics of plant diseases. Here are some alternatives:

**Wild potato, wild rue, rue anemone.** This plans is indigenous to eastern North America, where it grows particularly in mountainous districts of Pennsylvania. The roots are used as food locally. Perennial.

**Asphodel.** A member of the lily family, this species was widely cultivated in Roman times and was eaten by the Roman and Greek inhabitants of the empire just as we consume garden and farm potatoes today, as a common article of diet. Perennial.

**Kaffir potato.** The species yielding these tubers are found in southern Africa, notably Rhodesia, Natal and adjacent regions. They are eaten instead of ordinary potatoes and have a pleasant taste, being named locally *umbondive*. Perennial.

**Hausa potato.** A warm-area species, but may be grown in summer months in northern latitudes. Often cultivated and eaten as substitute for garden potatoes. Perennial.

**Potato bean.** Native to eastern North America, where it grows right down to Florida and Texas. It is a vine and bears sweet, edible tubers which may be boiled or roasted. Often cultivated. Potato beans are regarded as one of the best American wild food sources.

**Wood lily.** Another North American species, which yields edible bulbs, eaten in place of common potatoes. Indigenous to the northern states of the Mid-West. Perennial.

**Duck potato, arrowleaf, wapato.** This plant produces tubers similar to potatoes, which are eaten after boiling or roasting. Found in North and Central America. Perennial.

**Oca, ulluco.** A native of Bolivia, Peru and Colombia. It bears tubers, shaped like kidney potatoes, about 2 to $3\frac{1}{2}$ inches in length. The plants are of trailing habit and each node produces roots which enter the ground and bear the pseudo-potatoes. A crop will be mature and ready for harvesting some four months after planting, so it could be grown without difficulty in northern summers. Perennial.

**Caracu** and **yautia amarilla.** Here are two plants, called botanically *Xanthosoma caracu* and *Xanthosoma sagittifolium* respectively, indigenous to the West Indies and Central America. They also produce corms and are eaten as potato substitutes. Perennials.

**Tasmanian potato.** This plant bears kidney-shaped tubers, used instead of potatoes. There is a related species in New Zealand, the produce of which is consumed by Maoris. Perennials.

**Solanum species.**   Our ordinary common or garden potato belongs to the family *Solanaceae*. Many related species exist, which also provide edible tubers. Most of these plants are indigenous to the American continents and indeed out of the total number of *Solanum* species, only a few have been so far exploited and bred for large scale usage. Here are some other valuable types:

**Solanum andigenum.**   Grows in Peru and Colombia and bears good tubers.

**Solanum fendleri.**   Called popularly Findler potato, this plant is found in the south-western United States and from Mexico down to Panama. It bears palatable tubers.

**Solanum Jamesii.**   James' potato, a species common in the south-west of the United States and northern Mexico. Bears edible tubers.

FLOUR OR MEAL FOR BREAD, PORRIDGE AND CAKES

There are many plants which bear roots or underground parts that can be dried and ground into flour or meal. These then serve for making bread, cakes or porridge. Both sun-drying and artificial heat may be used to produce dehydration of the roots. After processing, the flours are mixed with water and other ingredients, according to the recipes chosen, and baked. In this way it is possible to provide effective substitutes for ordinary wheat flours or those of the different grain crops. Some useful species for making flour and meal are listed below.

**Abronia.**   A western North American plant, especially common in California. The dried roots can be milled into flour, which is used for baking or porridge. Perennial.

**Quackgrass.**   This plant possesses rhizomes and may be seen growing generally in northern temperate areas. After drying, the underground stems are ground up and the flour or meal can be used for bread and cake

making. Recommended as a useful food during times of scarcity. Perennial.

**Papago root.**   A species native to the south west of the United States and north-western Mexico. It bears large, succulent underground stems, which, after drying and grinding into flour, are used for bread making. The plant is pale and contains no chlorophyll.

**American sea rocket.**   This plant is found along the coastlines of North America. It has fleshy roots, which may be dried and ground into flour for bread. Perennial.

**Lilies.**   Different plants of the species *Calochortus*, indigenous to western North America, bear bulbs which, after drying, are ground into flour or meal and used for making porridge and gruel or bread and cakes. Amongst these are golden, bulbous, elegant and sagebush mariposa, mariposa lily or sego lily, and maiden lily. They are perennials.

**Cogswellia.**   Some five species of cogswellia plants, another native species of western North America, also furnish good roots which, when dried and milled, provide excellent flours for cake making. Perennials.

**Arrowroots** (*Curcuma* species).   Flours made from arrowroots are very delicate and digestible and make good porridge, puddings or cakes for invalids. Amongst useful types are East Indian arrowroot, native to the Himalayan region; Indian arrowroot from the eastern regions of India; false arrowroot, grown in Annam; and Amboinese arrowroot, originating in Java. These species are often cultivated. They bear large rhizomes, from which starchy flours are produced. All are perennials. The plants require warm and moist conditions and are propagated by division of the crowns or rhizomes. Partial shade is beneficial. They should not be confused with other arrowroots belonging to different species which are mentioned in this book.

**Dog's tooth lily.**   This plant grows in temperate Europe and northern Asia, extending as far as Siberia and Mongolia. The dried

22. Reed grass (*Phragmites communis*)

roots or bulbs provide flour, which is excellent for making vermicelli and cakes. Perennial.

**Mountain phellotrope.** A species native to New Mexico and Texas, this plant bears good roots which may be dried or baked and, after peeling, are ground into meal which is eaten in the form of porridge. Perennial.

**Reed grass.** A cosmopolitan type of plant which exudes a sweet substance from its rootstocks as a result of punctures caused by insects. The rhizomes are dried and then ground into flour. This contains appreciable amounts of sugar and makes an excellent porridge.

**Small Solomon's seal.** An eastern North American plant, this has a starchy rootstock and rhizomes which produce a useful flour. It has been recommended as a valuable emergency foodstuff. Perennial.

**Giant Solomon's seal.** Native to western North America, temperate Asia, and Japan.

The rhizomes are a source of starch and flour. Perennial.

**Douglas knotweed.** Another western North American species, the seeds of which can be ground into flour for making bread and porridge. Perennial.

**Beaverbread scurfpea.** A plant indigenous to the central United States and northern Mexico. The roots are dried and milled into flour which is used for baking bread or made into porridge and gruel. Perennial. It is a leguminous species.

**Common breadroot.** This grows in the eastern and southern United States. It has large turnip-shaped roots, which are rich in starch and can be milled into flour for making cakes and bread. Strongly recommended for cultivation. Perennial and leguminous species.

**Utah breadroot.** A similar species to common breadroot. Perennial and leguminous.

**Great bulrush.** Also called the club rush, this plant grows in North and Central America and the West Indies. The rhizomes are dried and milled into flour and used for making bread. Perennial.

**Nevada rush.** Of similar value to great bulrush. The roots provide a useful flour. Perennial.

**Marsh rush.** A North American plant, the rhizomes of which yield an excellent flour for baking bread. Perennial.

**Tuberous rush.** Also called *bateifun*, this plant grows in very moist conditions. It is used in China and Japan to produce a starch or flour for cakes. Perennial.

**Golden brier.** Native to eastern North America, the plant bears rhizomes which, when pounded and dried, provide flour for porridge. Lance or pointed brier is very similar. Both are perennials.

**Beyrich's brier.** Grows in the same areas as the golden brier and has tuberous rootstocks which yield an excellent flour for baking into bread. Hairy brier, false China brier and fat brier are very similar types. Perennials.

**Saw greenbrier**. This plant is known alternatively as bristly brier. It is found in the eastern and south-eastern United States. The large tuberous roots, after drying, provide a good flour or meal, suitable for bread making or porridge and gruel. Perennial.

**Laurel brier**. A plant of the south-eastern United States, this brier bears rootstocks which can be milled into flour or meal to provide a palatable porridge. Perennial.

**Long-stalked greenbrier**. A species of eastern North America, as well as the West Indies. The tubers are the source of a reddish-coloured flour much appreciated for porridge and cakes. Perennial.

**Tulips**. In times of emergency, tulip plants can make a useful contribution to food supplies. The bulbs of the edible tulip (*Tulipa edulis*), garden tulip (*Tulipa gesneriana*), and Cilician tulip (*Tulipa montana*) can all be consumed, usually by drying the bulbs and grinding them into flour, which can then be baked into bread and cakes, or cooked as porridge.

OTHER PLANTS FOR FLOUR AND MEAL PRODUCTION

The following species of plants can also yield useful flour for baking or cooking as porridge and gruel: chuno de concepcion – Chilean species with large roots; whitespot giant arum, Harmand's arum, and konjac, the source of konjaku flour; cannas, which yield African, Queensland and Brazilian or West Indian arrowroots; chestnuts; Moreth Bay chestnuts; chickpeas or garbanzos; dasheen; Australian arrowroot; different kinds of yams, such as the white, water, greater and ten-months yams, name de Agua, name Dunguey, Malacca yam, Chinese yam or potato, name de China, Madagascar yam, air potato, Guinea yam, yellow yam, Affun yam, negro yam, name Amarillo, name Guinea, cinnamon yam, Brazilian yam, kiwa, vigonjo, sinquekano, usumbura yam, potato yam, name papa, the lesser

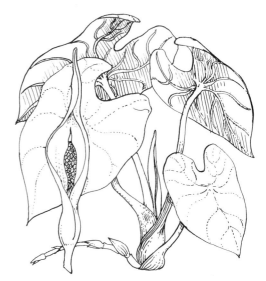

23. Dasheen (*Colocasia antiquorum* var. *esculenta*)

Asiatic, fancy, glandular, globe, heart-shaped, West Australian and akam yams, name akam, acom, luzon yam, light-skinned yam, maciba, Papua yam, sakai yam, spiny yam, wild yam, Queensland yam, yampi, name Mapicey, Morado, blaco yam, cushcush yam, cayenne yam; gleichenia fern, an Australian species with edible roots; various lilies with nutritious bulbs, such as the goldband lily, corded lily, dahurian lily, turep or oba-ubayuri, the lance, spotless, martagon, small-leaved, wood, pompon, sargent, turkcap and tiger lilies; yam-beans; Hawaiian and Fiji arrowroots, and Florida arrowroot, which has a thick underground stem.

ALTERNATIVES TO GARDEN CROPS

The general garden crops that we know so well include such types as parsnips, carrots, turnips, swedes, beetroots and kohlrabi. Substitutes for these plants can be found, without very much difficulty, growing wild. Here is a selection of useful species:

**Coralvine, mountain rose.** Grows naturally in Central and South America, or as a summer crop in temperate latitudes. Coralvine bears attractive tubers of nutty taste. Perennial.

**Great burdock.** A native of temperate Europe and Asia, but has been introduced into North America. The roots are eaten as a vegetable. Harvesting normally takes place in autumn and the produce can be stored for winter consumption. This plant prefers heavier soils. Perennial.

**Arracacha, arracha, Peruvian carrot.** Native to the Andean highlands of South America, from Venezuela to Bolivia, being a very important food amongst local peasants. The roots resemble parsnips and are used as a vegetable, though the flavour is slightly stronger but pleasant. Arracacha is also consumed in stews and soups, as well as being fried in slices. The species thrives at elevations of 7,000 to 8,000 feet above sea level in the Andes Mountains and can be cultivated during summer months in northern latitudes. Perennial.

**Abyssinian asparagus.** An Ethiopian plant, the large roots of which are fried for table use. It is eaten often in slices as an asparagus substitute. Perennial.

**Peta.** The roots of this plant are eaten as a vegetable in Peru. It supplies tasty and good-flavoured tubers. Perennial.

**Thistles.** Various species, notably the tuberous meadow thistle, indigenous to Europe, and other areas, supply edible roots. These are often recommended as emergency food. They can be stored during winter periods and are excellent boiled. Perennials.

**Earth nut.** A plant of the temperate regions of Asia and Europe. The starchy tubers are eaten as a vegetable and can sometimes be seen in markets. This is another useful food for times of scarcity or emergency. Perennial.

**Yampa.** Related to the earth nut, but indigenous to western North America, this species is a favourite food in many areas of the continent and was relished by Indian tribes. The roots can be eaten fresh or preserved for winter consumption. They have a very pleasant nutty flavour, making excellent vegetables. Other types similar to yampa are Kellogg's yampa and Oregon yampa. Biennial.

**Liquorice root.** This plant can be found growing from central Canada to Alaska. It is called liquorice root because the long, sweet roots resemble sticks of liquorice in appearance. They are sugary and make good spring vegetables. Perennial.

**Indian swede.** Another North American species, the roots of which taste like rutabaga or Swedish turnips. They can be cooked and eaten in similar manner. Perennial.

**Groundnut peavine.** Alternatively called earth chestnut, this plant is native to Europe and western Asia, but has been introduced into North America. The tubers may be boiled and eaten as vegetables. The roots are sometimes seen for sale in local markets in Syria and the Balkan states. Perennial and leguminous.

**Large evening primrose.** Found in Europe and North America, the large evening primrose bears roots which, when boiled, are eaten as a vegetable. It has been cultivated for food in certain areas. Biennial.

**Water parsley.** A species of the northwestern United States, which possesses black-skinned tubers of sweet, creamy taste and of excellent quality when cooked. Found along the Pacific coast. Perennial.

**Kudzu vine.** This plant is indigenous to China and Japan, but has been acclimatized in many other mild and temperate regions. The roots can be cooked and eaten as a vegetable. Perennial.

**Silverweed.** Another source of edible roots, silverweed grows in temperate parts of North America and Europe. It is common in damp, grassy and waste places. Perennial.

**Spanish oyster.** A species of the Mediterranean area. The roots are boiled and eaten as a vegetable. In past centuries the plant was commonly cultivated. Biennial.

24. Scorzonera (*Scorzonera hispanica*)

**Silky sophora.**  This is a North American plant which bears pleasant-tasting, sweet roots. They are considered a delicacy in New Mexico. Perennial.

**Giant bur reed.**  The tubers of this species make good vegetables. It is a North American plant. Perennial.

**Skunk cabbage.**  An eastern North American plant, which yields excellent tubers. Also termed swamp cabbage, the rhizomes can be dried and then baked for food. Biennial.

**Marsh woodwort.**  A European and North American species which yields palatable tubers for consumption as vegetables. Perennial.

**Columbine meadowrue.**  Found in Europe and northern Asia, this plant provides roots suitable for boiling or roasting. Perennial.

**Salsify.**  This species is cultivated in many areas for its roots, which have an oyster-like taste. They can be eaten fresh, after boiling, or stored for winter usage. There are a number of varieties, such as mammoth and Sandwich Island, of higher quality. Salsify roots resemble thin and slender parsnips. The plants prefer deep and rich soil. For table use, roots can be boiled whole, cut into slices or large pieces and fried in butter or grated and made into cakes. Annual to biennial.

**Viper's grass.**  Often called scorzonera, this species bears black-skinned roots. It is used in similar manner to salsify. Delicious scorzonera is the sweetest type, often cultivated in Sicily. Schweinfurth's scorzonera grows in the Egyptian deserts, the roots being consumed by local tribes. Good varieties of cultivated scorzonera are 'Vulcan' and 'Russian Giant'. Annual to perennial.

**Tuber nasturtiums.**  The edible nasturtium, the Patagonian nasturtium and the tuberous nasturtium or ysano supply tubers which make good vegetables. Sometimes cultivated and eaten boiled. Perennials.

**Marrowleaf cat tail.**  A cosmopolitan plant, the rootstocks of which form a valuable emergency foodstuff. The southern marrowleaf grows in Africa and has similar merits. Perennials.

**Bellwort.**  A North American plant, found in the eastern United States, which bears edible roots. Perennial.

**Edible valerian.**  Also a North American species, this plant is sometimes cultivated. The rootstocks make a good vegetable when boiled. Perennial.

**Atamasco lily.**  Found in the south of the United States. The bulbs are cooked and eaten. Perennial.

**Skirret.**  Also called chervin, this is a plant of the Mediterranean and eastern Asiatic areas. It was formerly much cultivated. The roots are consumed boiled. Perennial.

In addition to the plants listed above, there are

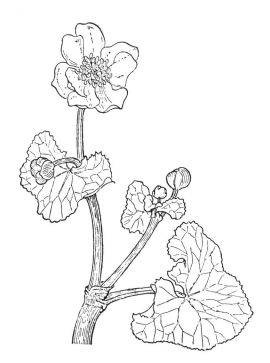

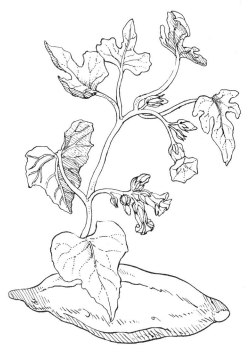

25. Marsh marigold (*Caltha palustris*)

26. Sweet potato (*Ipomoea batatas*)

numerous other types that produce palatable corms, tubers, roots, rhizomes and bulbs for consumption as vegetables. Amongst these we may mention briefly: yellow sandverbena, seacoast abronia, Californian abronia; broadleaf ladybell, Dahurian ladybell; Utah agave; Malayan, Indian and giant alocasias; Hooker's anchomanes; Jack-in-the-pulpit or Indian turnip, Hottentot turnip; macachi, found in Patagonia; arum, which needs boiling first to remove poisonous properties; butterflyweed; Canada milk vetch; Hopi vetch; baboon root; Puget and Hooker's balsamroots; Oregon sunflower or arrowleaf balsamroot; *Bomarea* species of Mexico, Santo Domingo, Chile and Ecuador; Madeira vine; Queensland bowenia; Niger fikongo; Brody's lily; tuberous chestnut; flowering rush; sweet corn root indigenous to the West Indies, where it was a principal food of the pre-Columbian inhabitants; finger poppy and pimple mallows; marsh marigold; calypso; calystegia; wild hyacinth, common camass; shiny canna; turnip-rooted chervil; rose elf or spring beauty; Alaska beauty; Carolina beauty; dazo; conanthera; Japanese, Siberian and Kalmuk corydalis; *Curcumas* of different types; Australian cymbidiums; gamote and globular gamote; chufa, earth almond or yellow nut grass; Indian almond; merkus; rattlesnake weed; various *Dioscorea* species, which bear edible tubers; Henderson's star; Australian earth chestnut; Tuareg root; Watling Street thistle; jicana; various fritillarias; edible gladioli; wild liquorice; habenarias of Amboina and south-western United States; oblonghead sunflower; Sioux artichoke; *Hoffmanseggia* and related species; shari

27. Bracken (*Pteridium aquilinum*)

icacina; different ipomoeas; edible iris, relished by the Arabs; laciniaria; tree mallow;
bitter root; penny flower; *Boscia*, South
African species; malabaila; Indian cucumber-
root; mertensia; Australian or Forster's scorzonera; Arizona monolepis; edible muscari;
different orobanches; goldenclub, the roots of
which need repeated boiling to remove the
acrid taste; Clayton's osmorhiza; various
*Oxalis* species; yambeans of assorted kinds;
Chinese peony; parosela; Langsdorff's ped-
icularis; Virginian tukkahoe or green arrow
arum; slender prairie clover; mountain phellopterus; edible polymnia; Queensland portulaca; bracken, used for its rhizomes; leafy-
stemmed false dandelion; Pallas' buttercup;
Brown's turnip or Mandingo turnip; columbine meadowrue; common tigerflower;
Japanese and Australian snakegourds; edible
*Typhonium* species of Australia; uvularia;

*Wyethia* species of western North America, the
roots of which are heated and fermented
before eating; yakhop; and zamias.

## Culture of Roots

Roots and tubers represent the chief stored
food reserves of biennial and perennial plants,
so it is obvious that for good formation and
development these organs will require adequate feeding. Moreover, the manurial programme or the soil should be capable of
providing a fair, all-round balance of nutrients. Thus, plentiful compost, organic waste
materials, farmyard manure, and similar substances, *well dug in*, or placed *deep down* in the
ground, are best. The reason why the fertiliz-
ing plant food should be at a good depth in the
soil is that roots should go straight down as
deep as possible, not look for much feeding at
surface level, otherwise the formation will be
branched, forked and irregular. This is not
attractive for table use and makes culinary
preparation more troublesome.

Superior results will be secured where soils
are deeper and reasonably loose. If they are too
stony, the roots or tubers may be obstructed.
Some root plants prefer alkaline land, others
like slightly acid conditions. Gardening books
list these differences. Roots demand ample
potash and phosphorus and the soil should not
be short of these essential elements. But
excessive nitrogen will encourage too much
foliage and leave the root parts consequently
smaller. These are important points to watch.

To obtain first-class roots and tubers,
gardeners and housewives will find the
following notes of value. Each class of crop has
been dealt with in turn.

### SUBSTITUTES FOR POTATOES

Many plants which provide alternatives to
potatoes develop their foliage comparatively
quickly. This is because the leaves must grow
to their full dimensions before the roots or

tubers attain a large size and call upon the bulk of the available supplies of nutrients. In most cases, care has to be taken to ensure that the underground tubers, roots or corms have an adequate covering of soil, otherwise damage may occur through overheating in hot regions, or greening and frost injury in cold localities. Root crops can often stand very warm weather provided the subterranean zone of the plants is kept cool. The same applies to winter conditions – harsh climatic effects can frequently be tolerated if the roots are well protected. Generally speaking, potato-substitute crops require ample supplies of potash, phosphates and iron. At the same time, the land should be free from waterlogging and generally can be slightly on the acid side. Excessive nitrogen should not be given, because it can cause the foliage to develop at the expense of the roots or tubers.

## FLOUR OR MEAL PRODUCERS

These roots are, of course, chiefly composed of starch or carbohydrate. Here again, the plants should receive only moderate amounts of nitrogenous manures or fertilizers, but should be allowed good supplies of potash and phosphates, as well as adequate calcium and magnesium. A substantial depth of soil for optimum production is desirable. Yams, in particular, require planting in small mounds or ridges of earth, with supports for the vines to climb up.

## ALTERNATIVES TO GARDEN CROPS

Beetroot types benefit from extra lime and potash and are helped by an occasional dressing of salt, unless the land is already on the saline side. For carrot substitutes, care must be taken to try and ensure that the soil is not too coarse or **very stony**. This can encourage splitting or forking of the roots. The same precautions apply to parsnip types of plants, which will generally need slightly more nitrogen than carrot substitutes.

## Cooking

Roots and tubers, or other vegetables of subterranean kinds, require good cooking if palatability and nutritive value are not to be lost.

Potato-type vegetables or potato substitutes contain much starch, which makes them a valuable source of calories in the diet. It is, however, essential to rupture the starch cells in cooking before the starch can be digested satisfactorily. Some vitamin C will be provided by these sorts of vegetables; a certain amount of second-class protein will also be available. For best results and dietary benefit, it pays to try as far as possible to boil or roast such vegetables in their skins, removing these after they are cooked if desired. Maximum flavour and food value will thus be obtained.

In general, root vegetables provide sugar in the diet, as well as some roughage, which has a laxative effect. The sugar is very soluble, so the produce should not be boiled in a lot of water or for a long time. The taste will also be affected if such a method is employed in the home. To preserve both the food value of the sugar and the taste of the vegetables, it is preferable to use conservative cooking methods.

The best way to cook is as follows. Clean and scrape the vegetables, or wash them well, using a small scrubbing-brush if they are to be cooked in their skins, then slice them thinly, if desired. Melt a little fat (butter or margarine or oil) in the pan and cook the vegetables in it, well below frying temperature and with the lid on the pan, for about ten minutes, until all the fat has been absorbed, shaking the pan occasionally. Then add carefully enough boiling water, with a pinch of salt, and simmer the vegetables gently until they are tender. Serve quickly while hot, with a little of the liquid remaining. You will now have excellent, well-flavoured vegetables of high food value. This way is superior to the old boiling method.

Many roots and tubers can be stored for winter or off-season use. It is also possible to dry them or reduce them to powder or grated forms for reconstituting with water when they are needed for consumption. Roots, cleaned and packed suitably, can be preserved in a freezer for long periods.

# Chapter 4

# SUBSTITUTES FOR MEAT

Because meat is generally looked upon as our chief source of proteins any good substitutes for this commodity must necessarily provide adequate quantities of these essential elements in our diet. The main supplies of proteins in plants may be found in those species that fall within the category of pulses. In dictionaries and reference books pulses are normally defined as plants of various leguminous types that yield seeds such as beans, peas and lentils, which when dried are used for food purposes. The English word pulse is derived from the Latin, *puls* or *pultis*, meaning porridge. This is not a bad description of the common appearance of these products when they have been cooked and prepared for the table.

It is not often realized that the legumes come near in importance to cereals as sources of human food. They provide more protein than do any other plants grown as vegetables and indeed in this respect they are superior to animal flesh and fresh fish. In addition, they supply carbohydrates and fats. The proteins occur in the form of small granules in the same cells with starch grains. As all gardeners and farmers know, legumes in most cases bear on their roots tubercules containing nitrogen-fixing bacteria, which are able to utilize free atmospheric nitrogen and convert it into nitrates. This augments the supply of nitrogenous material available for crops.

## Types of Pulses

Pulses, of which there are numerous types, have been collected, cultivated and eaten for many centuries all over the world. When dried, the seeds have a low-water content and their coats, or testas, are hard and impervious, which enhances their storage value and increases their keeping qualities. Growing pulses is not difficult; the plants mature rapidly and the products are highly nutritious, since apart from protein they also provide minerals and vitamin B. Moreover, they store well for long periods of time. For these reasons they may be looked upon as an absolute necessity in countries where meat is scarce, expensive or rarely consumed for different reasons.

In cold regions or where work performed involves the expenditure of considerable physical energy, pulses are especially important. Before the introduction, from the sixteenth century onwards, of the potato from the Americas into Europe and Asia, pulses formed a great part of the food of the poorer sections of the populations in those continents. Moreover, the plants' foliage provided excellent animal fodder, and when ploughed back into the soil constituted a valuable fertilizer.

It is therefore unfortunate that, despite their long history and important properties, pulses are rather neglected in many areas today. Gardeners and householders, as well as farmers, tend to forget the merits of these plants, or when they do grow them, concentrate mainly upon the common, better-known peas and beans for use simply as green vegetables. The production of dried pulses, which have higher food value, is virtually overlooked in many cultivation programmes. This is not to say that we should neglect the growing of green peas and fresh beans, which are excellent as general vegetables, but merely to emphasize the significance of the dried products. In addition, it is as well to remember that there are numerous species of pulses, for use both green and preserved, that are quite unknown nowadays to the average householder and gardener.

Today, when meat is expensive and may become even something of a luxury in future in households where it has hitherto been plentiful, the need for pulses is greater than ever. Because of their nutritional value, these leguminous seeds can offer satisfactory dietary substitutes for animal flesh. Indeed, some authorities consider that it is more healthy and beneficial to eat pulses than to consume the substantial quantities of meat that many people do now.

This argument on the respective merits of pulses and meats goes back very far in time. If we turn to the biblical *Book of Daniel*, Chapter 1, we can read an extremely interesting account of a test carried out on this particular point some 2,500 years ago. King Nebuchadnezzar of Babylon ordered that certain of the Jewish children captured at the fall of Jerusalem should be brought up in his palace and educated in the learning of the Chaldeans. Among these youngsters was Daniel. Together with his three friends, he refused to eat the meat and wine that were provided by the King's chief eunuch for their nourishment. Very upset, the eunuch said to Daniel:

'I fear my lord the king, who hath appointed your meat and your drink: for why should he see your faces worse liking than the children which are of your sort? Then shall ye make me endanger my head to the king.' Daniel replied: 'Prove thy servants, I beseech thee, ten days; and let them give us pulse to eat, and water to drink. Then let our countenances be looked upon before thee, and the countenance of the children that eat of the portion of the king's meat: and as thou seest, deal with thy servants.' So he consented to them in this matter, and proved them ten days. And at the end of ten days their countenance appeared fairer and fatter in flesh than all the children which did eat the portion of the king's meat. Thus Melzar took away the portion of their meat, and the wine that they should drink; and gave them pulse.

The above account of the effects of a diet based on pulses as compared with one composed of rich meat is taken directly from the Bible. In its simple and straightforward style it shows clearly how well these legumes can perform their purpose in keeping us fit and healthy.

Let us now consider some of the different kinds of leguminous plants, such as beans, peas, lentils and others that collectively come under the heading of pulses, which are less well-known but which have important uses and food values.

BEANS

Many types of beans exist which differ greatly in size, flavour and characteristics. Gardeners and housewives normally concern themselves mainly with common or runner beans, broad beans and French beans, little realizing that the lesser-known food beans can bring interesting variety into any dietary programme and add considerably to our intake of nourishment, as well as helping our home budget. Some useful species are given below.

**Sword, Jack or horse bean.** This is a robust, slightly woody perennial plant, with a climbing habit, but there is a dwarf type which does not exceed 2 feet in height. The plants are often grown as annuals. The pods are coarse, rather flat and sword-shaped, some

10 to 12 inches long and about $1\frac{1}{2}$ inches broad. They contain as many as twelve large white seeds. Some three hundred of these weigh about 1 lb. The unripe seeds and pods may be eaten sliced and boiled as a vegetable, or the pod alone can be sliced and the young and tender seeds cooked in the style of broad beans. If kept until mature, the beans may be dried and split, for use as a culinary pulse.

Climbing sword beans require poles or wires for support or can be allowed to grow up hedges, low spreading trees or fences. The dwarf type is bushy. In East Africa, this variety is known as the gotani bean. The plants are hardy and drought resistant and little troubled by pests. For cultivation, it is best to sow the seeds in rows about $2\frac{1}{2}$ feet apart with distances of $2\frac{1}{2}$ feet between each plant. From sowing to harvest takes some three months.

**Cluster or guar bean.** A bushy perennial species which grows from 2 to 4 feet tall and yields small, straight, radiating and hairy pods about 3 to 4 inches long, produced in clusters. For eating green, the pods must be picked very young. The ripe seeds vary in colour from black to grey and white, according to variety. Common in India.

**Lablab or bonavist bean.** This is a strong-growing bean, of perennial and climbing type. The pods are broad and flat, with warted or wavy margins, and measure about 4 to 5 inches in length. The plants are often treated as annuals. When young and tender, the pods may be eaten as a green vegetable. There are several varieties with white, pink or purple-coloured flowers and white or reddish seeds. The best kinds produce short and broad pods containing about two to three beans each. There is a bush or dwarf form of lablab bean which does not grow more than 2 to 3 feet tall and this is the most suitable for the household garden. One pound of beans, when dried, contains some 1,600 seeds. Lablab plants are also good for animal feeding.

**El-dhambala bean.** This is related to the lablab bean. It is a climbing type, bearing purple or mauve flowers and producing narrow, well-filled pods of about 3 inches in length.

**Madras bean.** Also called horse gram, this plant is a semi-erect annual species, from 2 to 3 feet in height, with narrow, curved pods of up to 3 inches long. It is grown extensively in drier areas as a food and yields an excellent pulse, with good protein and carbohydrate content. Madras bean is more oily and fibrous than lablab bean.

**Lentil.** This is one of our oldest food plants and also one of the most nutritious. Although originally indigenous to south-western Asia, lentils were introduced in early times into Greece and Egypt, as well as Mesopotamia. The plants are slender, tufted, and are many-branched. They are annuals bearing tendrils. Lentils grow up to 12 to 18 inches tall and produce short, broad pods with small lens-shaped seeds. This pulse is very digestible and is eaten, after cooking, as soup, gruel or porridge. The dried leaves and stems make excellent fodder. Lentils ripen about three months after sowing. If broadcast, some 30 lbs of seed will sow one acre, but when put into drills or lines, 15 lbs will suffice. Clay soils suit lentils best. They are rich in protein.

**Velvet, Lyon, Mucuna or Mauritius bean.** There are several names for this annual to perennial type of pulse. In fact, a number of closely-related species come under these categories, with many varieties. The beans are generally strong and quick-growing, of climbing habit and very fast development. The pods are velvety and curved, some 3 to 5 inches long, and contain dark brown or mottled, round seeds which cook and eat well after removal of the outer skin. The young pods are also edible, as well as the foliage. (*Illustrated overleaf.*)

**Potato or yam bean.** This is a vigorous climbing species, which produces good pods.

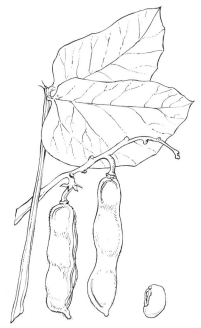

28. Velvet, Lyon, Mucuna or Mauritius bean (*Mucuna nivea*)

It also provides edible tubers. The pods are some 6 to 8 inches long and should be eaten when young as a vegetable, unless it is desired to keep the seeds for drying, in which case they may be allowed to reach maturity and ripen. To grow the potato bean, seeds should be placed in rows about 4 feet apart. When the plants come up, they are thinned out to 15 inches between each one. The climbing stems are supported on poles or wires or other convenient devices. Both blue and white-flowered varieties of these beans exist. The plants like warm and humid conditions in summer.

**Lima, Sieva, Java or Madagascar bean.** There are many varieties of these climbing beans. They are actually perennials, but in gardens are treated as annuals. The pods are short, fat and rather curved. The coloured seeded kinds contain traces of prussic acid and must be well washed and soaked before use, but the white varieties are free from this. Lima beans are of robust habit and contain a good amount of protein. The flowers are small and white, or pink in shade. Dwarf or bush varieties are preferable for household and garden use, since they do not require supports. Bush Limas attain a height of about 2 feet and are heavy croppers. Normally, they are sown in rows some 2 feet apart and cropping starts at six weeks after sowing, continuing for another month in favourable conditions. There are many excellent varieties available.

**Mung bean, green gram.** This comes in over one hundred varieties. The small, oval seeds are highly nutritious and the green pods can be eaten as a fresh vegetable. The plant is also utilized for fodder. An erect annual, growing to a height of some 16 inches, mung bean has narrow, cylindrical, straight and radiating pods about 3 inches in length. The leaves are trifoliate. The ripe seed is a very good pulse and is much eaten in India as 'dhal' or thin gruel and porridge. Drier conditions suit these beans best, but they will thrive at elevations of up to 6,000 feet above sea level in warm areas.

**Black gram.** This plant is a sub-species of mung bean and possesses longer stems and a more trailing habit. The seeds are fewer and darker in colour. Black gram is very highly esteemed. It can be eaten either in the form of bread made from a meal produced from the ground or milled seeds, or else boiled whole or in spiced balls. It is also the chief constituent of the thin wafer biscuits called papadams.

**Adsuki bean.** An important pulse much grown and used in China and Manchuria. These beans are often made into meal and paste, eaten in cakes and confectionary.

**Rice bean.** Common in southern Asia. Used in soups or boiled. Leaves also consumed.

**Moth or dew bean.** Often seen growing in India. An annual plant. Pods eaten fresh or seeds dried for later consumption.

**Winged, Goa, Manila or princess bean.** A strong-growing and climbing species, originally native to Mauritius, which bears peculiar four-angled pods and has large, pale blue flowers. The winged bean needs support in cultivation. The pods are up to 6 to 8 inches long and can be eaten when tender, after slicing and cooking. The plant also produces fleshy, tuberous roots at the rate of as much as 2 tons per acre. Seeds are normally sown in drills about 4 feet apart and allowed to climb on a wire fence or other support.

**Asparagus bean, yard-long bean.** This species is a twining annual, which bears long, pliant and narrow pods, up to 2 to 4 feet in length by $\frac{1}{2}$ inch broad. There are many varieties.

**Metcalf bean.** A drought-resistant species, this bean is a native of New Mexico and Arizona. It is sometimes cultivated. Foliage edible.

**Tepary bean.** Another drought-resistant type, the tepary bean is well-liked as a foodstuff, being prepared for culinary use in a number of different ways. There are many varieties and strains.

**Bean vine or wild bean.** Found in eastern and southern North American regions, this bean is highly esteemed. The seeds are dried and then eaten boiled.

**St Thomas bean or climbing entada.** The beans are eaten roasted and the young leaves consumed as a vegetable. Suited to warm, moist climates.

The seeds of the bean species mentioned above can be sprouted to provide a tasty, rapidly-produced vegetable dish. This is commonly done with mung beans and the well-known soya beans.

PEAS

The term peas relates not only to ordinary garden and field peas of the kinds familiar to the public, but also to various other species such as chick and cow peas or grams. It is not in any way a scientific definition, but a general word covering a list of edible seeds of small, rounded, pea-like shape.

**Pigeon pea, red gram or dhal.** This plant is a perennial and erect shrub, growing to 6 to 8 feet in height, with thin branches and narrow, trifoliate leaves. The seeds are dark grey or yellow, about the size of small peas, and are an important source of food. Pigeon peas are also notable for their value as forage. They are drought-resistant, tolerant of soils and mature rapidly. The seeds are very palatable. After drying and splitting, they can be eaten in soups, as gruel, or in the form of porridge. The plants may be grown in pure stands or in combination with other species. If pigeon peas are sown in rows, the distances between them should be generally 5 feet, with plants set out 4 feet from one another. The first harvest may be taken some six months after sowing. The bushes are cut back periodically and manured. Good varieties bear large pods, about 5 inches long. There are over thirty types of pigeon pea grown today.

**Chick pea or Bengal gram.** An annual pulse with small, pea-like angular seeds. Chick peas are very important in parts of Asia and Africa. The plants are branching and bushy in appearance and grow to about a foot in height. They were well known to the ancient Egyptians and Greeks. The sparse foliage should not be eaten, however, since it contains oxalic acid. There are about 3,000 seeds to the pound. The green pods are sometimes boiled to use as a vegetable. From sowing to harvest takes about ninety days and the plants tolerate dry conditions.

**Cow, Jerusalem, blackeye or catiang pea.** This species is a vigorous, bushy or trailing plant of annual type, with trifoliate leaves. The pods are cylindrical and pendant, about 4 to 6 inches long. Cow peas are a very ancient crop, being known in south-eastern Asia for over 2,000 years and in the United States since the eighteenth century. The seeds

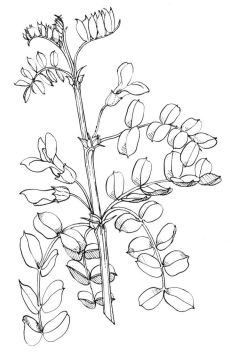

29. Pea tree (*Caragana arborescens*)

Seed

30. Vetch (*Vicia sativa*)

constitute a good pulse food, while if desired the pods can be eaten as a green vegetable, being sliced like French or runner beans. The species prefers a sandy or loamy soil. Dry seeds are rich in protein.

**Kudzu.**   A perennial cropper, with a long tap root and runners up to 100 feet in length, the kudzu vine provides edible leaves and shoots. It thrives on depleted soils and will renovate exhausted land. The pods and seeds can also be consumed.

**Field pea.**   This pulse probably originated from the grey pea, which can be seen growing wild in Greece and the Near East. The seeds are angular and the flowers coloured. The field pea is hardy, withstands frost and thrives up to 8,000 feet above sea level. The seed is split and used for split peas or peameal. The whole plant is excellent for feeding purposes, as well as being rich in protein. Various kinds are available for different purposes. Drying strains are best for split peas. Speckled varieties, the black-eyed Susan type, and dun and brown-coloured peas with a black mark or eye, are excellent.   There   are   also   others   with small bluish-green seeds and dimpled bigger kinds. Bavarian winter pea, black-podded pea, capuchin pea, smyrna pea, gray konigsberger pea, East Prussian pea, paluschke pea and sand pea are included within the category of field peas.

**Pea tree.**   The alternative name for this shrub or small tree is Siberian pea shrub. It bears edible pods which are eaten green as a vegetable. The plant is indigenous to Siberia and is leguminous.

OTHER SPECIES

**Vetches.**   These plants possess trailing habits in general and so it is often a good plan to grow them interspersed in a taller crop, so that they can climb up the stalks of the bigger and straight species. The seeds of vetches may be eaten as pulses. Numerous species exist including bard vetch, Hungarian vetch, common vetch, hairy vetch, Gerard vetch, kidney vetch, monantha vetch, with seeds similar to lentils, Narbonne vetch, one-flowered vetch, and Russian vetch. Vetch seeds should be soaked in water before use.

**Vetchlings.** These belong to the various *Lathyrus* species. Many types are used for human food, particularly the Chiptewa and Ojibway vetchlings, the Nebraska vetchling, and the New Mexican vetchling, as well as the maritime vetchling of Alaska. Grass pearine and plat pea are also edible, but the seeds must be well soaked in water before use.

**Sweet lupine.** This plant does not carry the bitter toxic principle that ordinary lupines do. It thrives on poorer land. The seeds are edible and palatable.

**Egyptian lupine.** This plant bears seeds which are eaten in Egypt. Very similar is the white lupine, which was consumed as a foodcrop by the Romans.

## Culture of Pulses

Pulse plants supply most of their own nitrogen needs and excessive manuring with this element is likely to depress yields rather than to increase them. Phosphate and potash are important and the soil should, generally speaking, not be too acid (except for lupins). Lime is a good stimulant for beans. Farmyard manure and well-prepared composts are excellent, whether on light or heavy soils. Too-rich conditions will cause the plants to produce much haulm, or foliage, and fewer seeds, which is not desirable. Householders and gardeners should therefore aim to supply only enough manure or fertilizer to ensure that the plants are properly but not excessively nourished. All pulses are very suited to inclusion in rotations, especially after cereals or roots. In gardens, it is most advantageous to intercrop or interplant pulses with other vegetables or grains. This not only saves space but provides extra nitrogen in the soil for leafy species, such as salads, cabbages or spinach.

Beans, peas and other pulses are harvested when the tops or haulms are turning brown and the seeds pods are ripe, unless it is desired to eat the pods green as a fresh vegetable. After threshing or removal of the seeds, the foliage can be fed to livestock. The seeds should be dried carefully and stored in suitable conditions until required for consumption.

These crops normally require good aeration of their roots and should never be allowed to become waterlogged. Their need for nitrogen is not as high as it is for non-leguminous plants, but it should be remembered that sufficient phosphates, potash and sulphur are essential for the good growth of pulses. Potassium sulphate, applied fortnightly, is a very satisfactory garden dressing, especially when supplemented by superphosphate.

## Cooking

Pressure cooking is excellent for pulses, since it saves much time. To obtain the best results, the following rules should help:

(a) Always soak the dried pulse seeds, except lentils, for about half an hour in water or any other cooking liquid before putting them on the stove to cook;

(b) When using a pressure cooker, put the pulses straight into the pan – do not use the rack;

(c) Add two pints of cold water and one level teaspoonful of salt to each $\frac{1}{2}$ lb of pulses. Bring to the boil in the open pan, then reduce the heat and cover with a lid for the rest of the cooking period;

(d) With a pressure cooker, build up slowly to 15 lbs pressure. Cook all beans and whole dried seeds for some 20 minutes and split peas and lentils for about 15 minutes. Reduce the pressure slowly.

Cooking times for pulses in ordinary pans fitted with lids are:

|  | *Minutes* |
|---|---|
| Dried peas or softer seeds | 25 |
| Split peas | 30 |
| Softer beans | 45 |
| Harder beans and seeds | 60 |
| Lentils (unsoaked) | 25 |

In ordinary cooking, pulses should be soaked in water overnight or for about eight to twelve hours before putting them on the stove. When cooking, put the pulses into fresh, cold water, add salt, and then bring to the boil. Cook gently until soft. The times given above may have to be lengthened in cases where pulses have been stored in very dry conditions, or where the water is too hard. The flavour of pulses will be improved and enhanced if one or two bay leaves are put into the water and boiled along with the seeds. A little butter may be added at serving time, or a suitable sauce provided.

Many excellent and interesting recipes have been devised for pulses. In particular mention may be made of Boston baked beans, pease pudding, lentil pie, purée and soup, chick pea porridge (with olive oil and parsley), bean pie, pea purée, bean curd, all types of sprouted pulses for salads and other dishes, various Spanish, Italian, Mexican and Levantine preparations of chick peas, rissoles of beans, the Greek fasoulia, the Arab *hummus bi tahima*, and other tasty and appetizing recipes. Full details of all these can be found in reputable cookery books. After grinding into meal or flour, pulses provide the means of making excellent and nourishing biscuits.

## Preserving

Pulses can be quick-frozen if the pods and green seeds are picked and packed for keeping in the freezer. For storing dry pulses it is essential to ensure that the beans, peas or other produce are properly dried and free from dirt or excessive moisture. This dehydration can be carried out by placing the seeds in sunshine in hot areas or in slow ovens or by warming on drying-racks in damp and cold localities.

# Chapter 5

# ALTERNATIVES TO ONIONS AND TOMATOES

Cooking and the preparation of food would indeed be uninteresting and unappetizing in the absence of those firm favourites onions and tomatoes. Not only would we be unable to enjoy well-flavoured salads, soups, and stews, but we would miss all the tasty sauces and gravies to which we have been accustomed for so long. Happily, it is possible to find acceptable substitutes for the ordinary garden onion and tomato. In addition, there are plants that can be used in place of those related species – leeks and garlic – that help to make our daily menus palatable.

Onions have been eaten by human beings since the very earliest times. We can read in the biblical book of *Numbers* how the Is-raelites, suffering in the desert of Sinai, bewailed their lot and murmured against Moses, saying: 'We remember the fish, which we did eat in Egypt freely; the cucumbers, and the melons, and the leeks, and the onions, and the garlic: but now our soul is dried away: there is nothing at all, beside this manna, before our eyes.' This absence of onions and leeks, amongst other shortages, sparked off a serious rebellion.

Tomatoes, until the sixteenth century, were unknown to Europeans, Asians and Africans. Only in the Americas did the pre-Columbian inhabitants enjoy the pleasure of consuming these garden fruits. For many years after their introduction to the Old World, however, tomatoes, or love-apples as they were termed, did not attain any great popularity and were regarded as a curiosity and a luxury of little general interest or value.

Only during the current century, with the advent of improved cultural techniques which have succeeded in making tomatoes available to the public all the year around, have these delicious plant products become essential to housewives and cooks. They are regarded today as vital to good diets and menus, and we should all miss them greatly should they suddenly disappear without any satisfactory replacements.

## Substitutes for Onions

There is quite a number of lesser-known plants that can provide alternatives for onions in our diet. Here are some suggestions:

**Akaka.**   A Persian species, which also grows in other parts of temperate Asia. Perennial.

**Siberian onion.**   Grows in Siberia. Often stored for winter usage. Perennial.

**Tree or Egyptian onion.**   This produces marble-sized bulbils on the flower stalks. Offset bulbs are also formed underground. (*Illustrated overleaf.*)

**Cibol, stone leek.**   Indigenous to Siberia. It is used as an annual or perennial. Suitable as 'spring onions' or for bulbs.

**Lady's leek or nodding onion.**   The bulbs are strongly-flavoured and make excellent soups. Also used for pickling. Perennial.

**Royal salep.**   Eaten in Persia and Afghanis-tan. A native of Central Asia. Perennial.

31. Tree or Egyptian onion (*Allium cepa*, var.)

**Ainu onion.**   A Japanese species. Popular in salads.

**Chinese chive or fragrant onion.**   Used for flavouring, this has a delicate aroma. Grows from Siberia to China and Japan. It is considered to have a purifying effect upon the blood. Perennial.

**Assam onion.**   A native of eastern India, used amongst the hill peoples. Perennial.

**Longroot onion.**   Found in Europe, northern Asia and Japan. Perennial.

**Splendid onion.**   A popular Japanese species. The bulbs are small, but are eaten boiled or pickled in vinegar. Perennial.

**Ballhead onion.**   Grows in Europe and temperate Asia. Much eaten by the people of the Lake Baikal area in Siberia. Perennial.

**Wild leek.**   A North American species, often used for flavouring dishes. Perennial.

**Japanese onion.**   Grows in Japan, temperate Asia and Europe. Bulbs are eaten as a vegetable. Perennial.

**Shallot, ascalon onion.**   Often cultivated. It seldom produces seeds and is propagated by separating the small bulbs. Perennial.

**Multiplier onion.**   Similar to the shallot.

**Welsh onion.**   A type of 'spring onion'.

Onion types prefer light, open soils, fairly well enriched, and the best bulbs are secured when they grow near the surface of the ground.

## Substitutes for Leeks

Leeks have a milder flavour. Several species, listed below, can be eaten instead of the ordinary garden type.

**Meadow or rose leek.**   Also called Canada garlic or wild garlic, this is native to North America, growing in the eastern states, as far south as Florida and Texas. It can be boiled or pickled. Perennial.

**Levant garlic.**   A Mediterranean species. The plants are popular in southern Europe. Perennial.

**Sand leek, roundheaded leek, few-flowered leek, three-cornered leek.**   Wild species with odour and taste of common leeks. The sand leek is cultivated in central and southern Europe and Asia Minor, but is regarded as a weed in the British Isles.

**Stone leek.**   Bears good-flavoured leaves. Perennial.

## Substitutes for Garlic

As regards garlic, there are a number of substitutes available:

**Giant garlic.**   Found in southern Europe and Asia Minor. Perennial.

**Twisted leaf garlic.**   A Siberian plant, sometimes cultivated. Perennial.

**Canada garlic.**   A North American species. Perennial.

**Crow garlic, field garlic, keeled garlic and rosy garlic.** All these plants possess suitable aroma and pungency.

**Ramsons.** A broad-leaved garlic. Pungent odour.

## Substitutes for Tomatoes

The tomato is a member of the family *Solanaceae* and though the species is in many ways distinctive, it is possible to find alternative fruits that can replace it in cooking and general dishes. The following plants possess similar attributes.

**Children's tomato.** This is an African species, the tomato-type fruits of which are eaten in sauces and soups and can be dried and preserved. It is sometimes cultivated.

**Fidji tomato.** A Polynesian type, frequently cultivated. The fruits are red, greatly resembling garden tomatoes. Eaten locally.

**Alkekengi.** Native to central and southern Europe and the area of the Ural Mountains. The berries are small, about the size of a cherry, and the plant has been cultivated. The calyx surrounding the fruits should not be eaten. Perennial.

**Ground cherry.** A North American species, the fruits of which can be eaten raw or made into sauce. Annual. Very similar types are Findler's cherry, lance-leafed cherry, New Mexico cherry, viscid cherry and Virginian cherry.

**Sun berry.** A tropical type, the fruits being eaten as a vegetable. Perennial.

**Strawberry-tomato, downy ground cherry, dwarf cape-gooseberry.** This plant is found in the Americas, the West Indies, Europe and Asia. It is a low kind of annual. The berries make a good sauce and can be used in cooking.

**Kangeroo-apple.** An Australian plant. When fully ripe the fruits can be eaten raw, baked or boiled. Perennial.

**Pepino.** Found in Central and South America. The fruits are often seedless and are round to long in shape and of greenish-yellow colouring with purplish-red blotches. Pepino has an agreeable taste and is juicy and slightly aromatic. Perennial. A subtropical species.

**Tree tomato.** A popular plant in Peru, but also introduced into subtropical and tropical areas elsewhere in the world. The fruits are oval or egg-shaped, smooth, of reddish-yellow hue and have an agreeable taste. They may be eaten raw or used in cooking. Small tree.

**Hartweg's berry.** Another South American plant, which bears reddish berries. These are used in local cooking and can be seen in the markets of Colombia, the Argentine and Chile. Perennial.

## Culture of Onion and Tomato Substitutes

Onion and tomato substitutes, as well as alternatives to garlic and leeks, can in general be grown with little trouble in all parts of the world, provided the area chosen is suitable to the needs of the particular species of plants and suitable climatic protection can be given, or the types selected are raised during summer periods in cooler localities. Onion substitutes prefer lighter, open kinds of soils, while most tomato-resembling plants thrive best when provided with richer, but well-drained ground. In both cases, however, and this also applies to leeks and garlic, care should be taken not to over-feed the plants, since this will encourage development of excessive foliage at the expense of the fruits, stems or bulbs.

The main objects of tilling or digging and cultivating the soil are to loosen the ground and so facilitate the absorption of moisture, permit the penetration of fresh air – that is to say, oxygen – and to control the growth of any competing plants. Tillage in gardening should aim at maintaining a proper water supply in the land, ensuring that it is permeable to rain or irrigation, and encouraging the activity of soil bacteria. In addition, cultivation assists the good effects of manuring and fertilization.

Although it is true that, in natural conditions, no digging occurs, and the plants compete against one another in the struggle for water, food, and survival, resulting in the victory of the fittest and strongest, yet for gardeners and householders, this would not always be the best and most efficient system. Of course, where there are large stands of edible plants growing wild we can collect their produce without any work at all, other than the labour of picking and harvesting. However, we may not be always lucky enough to find such abundance of natural produce nearby, so we have to keep gardens. In these, for ease of work and high output, we must protect our plants from competition and give them ample nutrition and adequate care.

This is applicable especially to onion and tomato substitutes. In dry areas much can be achieved by using level culture – that is to say, flat beds and not ridges – by packing the soil with a roller, and by practising deeper sowing. When planting, the earth should be pressed around seedlings or small bulbs. In wet areas, the growing-beds can be raised up above ground level to secure more efficient drainage. Shelter from wind, as well as shading from scorching sun in tropical areas, aids fruit formation. In cold regions, protection and heat must be provided for tender plants, should it be desired to produce vegetables during winter periods.

Most onion-type plants need reasonably dry conditions around the bulbs or corms. They consume quite substantial quantities of potash and nitrogen manures or fertilizers. Waterlogging is highly undesirable. In general, the best procedure is to allow the tops to die down and then harvest the mature produce, after it has ripened fully. In the cases of leek substitutes, the plants are normally gross feeders and must receive relatively large

amounts of nitrogen, potash and phosphates. For really tender vegetables of a good colour, the stems may be blanched by putting plastic collars around them.

Tomato types are, of course, valuable for the fruits they bear. Here, we are concerned with securing as little foliage as possible and the maximum number of 'tomatoes'. Fruits are delicate and therefore protection from wind, heavy rain, frost or snow helps to obtain the best specimens. This can be achieved by using shades in hot regions or culture under glass in cold areas. During the earlier stages of growth plants will use more nitrogen, but this should be cut down during the middle and later periods, when adequate potash, phosphates and iron are most essential. Excessive nitrogen at such times will lead to production of a lot of leaves at the expense of fruits. Good results may be secured by germinating seeds in boxes and subsequently transplanting the young seedlings into their permanent positions.

## Cooking

Onion and leek substitutes can be used in salads and cooked dishes where normally onions would be used for flavouring, or as a vegetable. Alternatives to tomatoes can fulfil a similar role in menus. In addition, they may be very serviceable in making sauces, and for flavouring. Because modern tomato hybrids, which form the bulk of the produce sold in the town and suburban shops and markets today, are very tasteless, the piquancy and exotic merits of the tomato substitues listed in this chapter should be much appreciated by housewives and their families.

When preparing tomato substitutes, treat them more or less as standard tomatoes. They can be sliced, boiled, fried or used in soups and stews. If you wish to remove the skins the easiest way to do this is to pour boiling water over them and leave them to stand for a few minutes. The skins will then peel off readily. In making sauces and preserves or chutneys, follow the normal recipes in your cookbook, but replace the tomato ingredient with the particular substitute you are using.

Onion and garlic or leek substitutes may also be treated in similar manner. Often, wild plants of the species listed above may be found growing in hedgerows, woods or fields in the local neighbourhood. Only collection is necessary. The pungent odour that these plants give off aids recognition.

All the substitutes mentioned here may be preserved by quick freezing in the usual way.

# Chapter 6

# STAFFS OF LIFE

Dry grains and seeds are without doubt probably the most important sources of plant food available to man, constituting as they do the staffs of life upon which the human race leans. We all know that cereals, such as wheat, maize, barley, sorghum, oats and rye provide us with our daily bread or bread substitutes. The ancient Romans and Greeks revered the goddess Ceres, the giver of grain, after whom cereals are named. Indeed, the name Ceres is derived from the Latin *creare*, to create. The Aztecs of Mexico also worshipped the corn goddess; images of her could be bought in the markets so that a farmer might bury it in his field with prayers for a good harvest. Every early civilization paid homage to some similar deity to watch over their crops.

Today, science has replaced the grain gods and goddesses of olden times and has succeeded in improving and perfecting our cereal crops almost beyond recognition. New so-called 'miracle' wheats and rices, as well as superior maize, give greatly enhanced yields and have been acclaimed in some quarters as the pillars upon which rests the 'Green Revolution' – that term popularly applied, chiefly by the media, to the agricultural innovations of the 1950s and 1960s which promised vast increases in food output. In fact, not long ago, we were being informed by noted authorities that the new miracle grains, supports of the Green Revolution, had put fears of famine away for ever.

Alas, as many knowledgeable scientists, farmers and gardeners have always been aware, these claims were largely false and rested upon unsure foundations. The new miracle grains demand very high standards of care, excessive quantities of artificial fertilizers, water in abundance and vast amounts of poisonous pesticides, together with special cultivation techniques. Far too often the costs of production are too great for the small farmer to undertake. Should one of these items – pesticides, fertilizers or care – be missing, the new crops may fail. These new hybrids are also especially prone to disease unless adequately protected. These are the weak and defective links in modern agricultural methods.

Consequently, the Green Revolution's promises and claims have not been fulfilled, and there is a real danger that it may recoil on us in an unpleasant way. This all emphasizes the great importance of turning our attention towards the many lesser-known grain and seed plants, not often grown or used, as standbys in times of emergency and as useful producers of food that we can consume in our households and neighbourhoods. Should epidemic diseases strike the common agricultural cereal crops, wiping out the hybrid plants, we can fall back on the lesser-known dry grains and seed species to fill the gap and save the situation.

In addition, householders and gardeners can easily grow plots of many of these lesser-known species to give valuable home stocks of grain for providing flour and meal for bread, cakes, porridge and other cooking needs. They often thrive on poorer soils or in harsher conditions, grow more rapidly and require less care and attention. The value of the lesser-known dry grains and seeds is very considerable and it is a great pity that they are so frequently neglected or overlooked in garden programmes, or that the collection of their produce from natural stands is not undertaken.

## Important Types of Dry Grains and Seeds

One interesting and useful attribute of many of the lesser-known dry grains and seeds eaten for food is that they may generally be grown as catch crops, thus providing a quick and helpful supply of nutriment at convenient periods. Here are some names of noteworthy types, which can be cared for with little difficulty.

**Amaranths.**   Well-known as green vegetables, but also yield appreciable amounts of edible seeds, which provide excellent food. These seeds may be white, yellowish or black in colour. The best and biggest species are given below, though the list is not exhaustive.

**Prostrate amaranth.**   A plant of western North America, the seeds of which can be eaten as pinole. There are five species closely related to prostrate amaranth also growing in the same region with very similar properties. Perennials.

**Inca wheat, quinoa, quihuicha.**   A species cultivated in various areas, notably Africa, South America and eastern India. The seeds are ground into flour and used for making bread. Annual.

**Ganges amaranth.**   Belongs to warmer areas. Seeds edible. Perennial.

**Australian amaranth.**   Seeds are used as food in Central Australia. Perennial.

**Slim amaranth.**   A plant of the temperate zone. Often cultivated, the seeds being milled into flour or meal. Annual.

**Redroot amaranth.**   This species is also called pigweed and green amaranth. It is native to temperate regions. The seeds are used as food. Annual.

**Lamb's quarters, fat hen.**   This belongs to temperate areas and produces seeds which are used, after milling, to make flour for cakes, bread and porridge. In appearance, the plant is erect and bears toothed leaves and inconspicuous flowers of green colour. The flavour of the seeds resembles that of buckwheat. Annual.

**Quinoa.**   A South American species, which attains a height of about 5 feet. The leaves are glaucous and powdery grey underneath. The seeds are small and shining. They must be soaked and steeped in water to remove the bitter property, then they are dried and ground into flour. Quinoa is very nutritious, containing thirty-eight per cent protein. The flour is used for bread, porridge and cakes and the seeds can be made into soups, or into a beverage called *tschitscha*. Annual. This species should not be confused with Inca wheat (see above) which also bears the alternative name of quinoa.

**Fremont's goosefoot.**   Found in western North America. The seeds are ground into flour in Oregon and often mixed with corn meal for porridge and for baking purposes. Perennial.

**Mimosas, acacias, wattles.**   Many of these species yield pods and seeds which can be dried, milled into flour and used for baking bread. In particular, the prairie acacia, a plant indigenous to the southern United States and Mexico, several Australian acacias, the giraffe acacia of South Africa, the umbrella acacia, another Australian species, and seyal acacia are noted for their produce. Small trees.

**Soulkhir.**   A species of Mongolia and Siberia. The seeds are an important food, which can be milled into flour. Annual.

**Large cane or southern cane.**   Found in the eastern and southern parts of North America.

32. Wild oat (*Avena fatua*)

The seeds are used as a substitute for wheat. Perennial.

**Persian milk vetch.**   The seeds are eaten as food in some parts of Iran. A species native to the Middle East and North Africa. Perennial.

**Four-wing saltbush.**   A shrub of western North America and Mexico. The seeds are edible and were eaten by Indian tribes.

**Wild oat.**   This plant can be seen growing wild in Europe, Asia and North America. The seeds can be made in flour for bread, cakes, or porridge. Perennial.

**Naked oat.**   Probably originated in southern Europe, but found in many areas today. Sometimes cultivated. Seeds or grains used flour and meal. Annual.

**Hungarian oat.**   Similar to naked oat. Sometimes seen in cultivation. Annual.

**Puget balsamroot.**   Indigenous to western North America. The seeds are made into bread. Perennial.

**Japanese sloughgrass.**   This plant grows in temperate Asia and North America. The grains are eaten in Japan. Perennial.

**Job's tears.**   A grass bearing large, shining, pear-shaped grains. It attains a height of 1–3 feet and has broad leaves. Job's tears thrives in the same conditions as does maize or corn. The seeds are milled into flour. There are several varieties under cultivation. Annual.

**Hausa millet.**   This is an African species, cultivated sometimes for its cereal grains. Used for making flour and meal. Annual.

**Iburua millet.**   Similar to Hausa millet and also grown as a cereal grain. Annual.

**Shama millet, jungle rice.**   This plant prefers warm conditions. It is often cultivated. Annual.

**Sanwa millet, Japanese millet, billion dollar grass.**   An annual grass, native of east Asia. It bears edible seeds.

**Egyptian millet.**   Grows in the tropics and sub-tropics. Seeds are eaten after grinding into flour. Perennial.

**Korakan, African millet.**   Another warm-area species, originally native to India. The seeds are made into a meal called ragi flour, used in cakes, puddings and porridge. Annual.

**Abyssinian millet.**   Found in some parts of Ethiopia, this plant bears seeds or grains used for flour and meal. Annual.

**Giant wild rye.**   Indigenous to western North America, this plant produces seeds suitable for milling into flour for bread making. Perennial.

**Wild wheat, wild beardless rye, squaw grass.**   Another western North American type. The seeds or grains are ground into flour and eaten in porridge or cakes. Perennial.

**Nevada joint ephedra.**   Found from Nevada to California in the western United States, this plant bears seeds which, after roasting, are milled into flour and made into bread. Stated to be beneficial for urogenital complaints. Shrub.

**India wheat, tatary, Siberian buckwheat.**    The seeds are a source of flour. It is native to northern Asia. Annual.

**Sugar grass, mamma grass.**    A North American plant, the seeds are used there as food. It is also found in Europe and Asia. Perennial.

**Niger seed.**    After pressing, the seeds of Niger oil or werinnua oil plants can be mixed with honey or sugar and made into cakes. Perennial. Suited to warm climates.

**Egyptian barley.**    Grown in Asia Minor and North Africa, this cereal plant yields a flour used for baking bread and cakes. Annual.

**Desert pepperweed.**    Found in the south-western areas of the United States. The seeds are used as a foodstuff. Semi-shrub.

**African sprangletop.**    This plant grows in Africa and Australia. The seeds can be used as an emergency foodstuff in times of scarcity. The grass is also an important fodder. Perennial.

**Rocky Mountain flax.**    The seeds can be ground into flour and used for various purposes in cooking. A western North American species. Perennial.

**Lupines.**    The white lupine was grown as a food crop by the Romans. The European yellow lupine seeds, when fresh, contain a poison, which must be removed by a special process before they can be eaten. The Egyptian lupine, an annual species, bears seeds which are eaten in North Africa and sold in markets.

**Bengal chestnut.**    A woody grass species, found in East Bengal or Bangladesh and Burma. It bears large mealy edible seeds, resembling chestnuts, which can be dried and made into flour or eaten roasted. Perennial.

**White mentzel.**    Indigenous to western and south-eastern parts of the United States. The seeds are made into a parched meal used locally as foodstuff. Annual to perennial.

**Montana grass.**    Found in western North America, this grass bears edible seeds or grains. Perennial.

**Cockspur grass.**    The alternative name for this plant is kheri. It is native to the temperate areas of the world and bears seeds which can be milled into flour, making excellent cereal-type porridge or dumplings, often eaten in Japan. The species is erect and quick-maturing. Annual.

**Native millet or umbrella grass.**    An Australian species, which produces good grains or seeds. When ground into meal these make an excellent foodstuff. Perennial.

**Proso millet.**    Found in the temperate zones and northern India. The seeds are made into flour, used in bread. The plants attain a height of from 2 to 3 feet. Annual.

**Vine mesquite.**    A species of western United States and Mexico, this perennial grass bears seeds which are ground into meal for porridge and bread.

**Texas or Colorado millet.**    Indigenous to south-western regions of the United States. Sometimes grown for its seeds. Annual.

**Little millet.**    A tufted grass, with edible seeds, suitable for making flour. Annual.

**Koda millet.**    This plant grows to about 4 feet in height. The seeds or grains must be well washed in water and dried before milling into flour. Several varieties are available. Perennial.

**Sahara millet.**    Indigenous to North Africa, especially drier areas. It bears seeds or grains often used for food. Perennial.

**Bulrush millet.**    This plant has broad leaves and attains a height of from 4 to 6 feet. The grain is used to make flour or meal. Suited to warmer regions and thrives in conditions appropriate to maize or corn. Perennial.

**Canary grass.**    Found in the Mediterranean region, but introduced into other areas. It can be eaten by human beings, after milling into flour, and also has importance as a commercial bird-seed. Annual. (*Illustrated overleaf.*)

**Sonora mesquite.**    A small tree of Arizona,

33. *Left*: canary grass (*Phalaris canariensis*)
34. Foxtail millet (*Setaria italica*)

Sonora, and South California, which thrives in dry conditions. The seeds may be milled into flour or meal and cooked as porridge or cakes.

**Teff grass.**   An East African species, grown as a cereal in some areas. There are varieties with black and white grains. Suitable for making flour. Annual.

**Douglas knotweed.**   A species of western North America, found especially in the states of Oregon and Washington. The seeds are made into flour. Perennial.

**Mountain rye.**   This cereal is found in southern Europe, North Africa, Asia Minor and the Middle East. There are western and eastern groups of varieties, some being annual and others perennial rye grasses. Mountain rye is grown as a grain crop.

**Tibetan rye.**   This plant thrives in the hilly areas of Tibet and China, so is most resistant to cold. The grains or seeds are used as food. Annual to perennial.

**Thistle sage.**   A Californian plant, often seen in the south-west United States. The seeds are roasted and ground into flour. Perennial.

**Chia.**   A Mexican species, often cultivated. Perennial.

**California chia.**   Indigenous to western North America, where the seeds are parched and milled into dark-coloured flour used for bread and cakes. Both the ordinary chia and the California chia are made into popular cooling drinks. The California chia is an annual.

**Foxtail millet.**   Indigenous to Europe and Asia and cultivated in many areas. There are a number of good varieties, such as Golden Wonder, Hungarian, Siberian and Kursk. The seeds are used as cereals and ground into flour. Annual.

**Pignut, goatnut.**   Found in southern California and northern Mexico. The seeds can be roasted and ground into flour. When this is mixed with the yolk of hard-boiled egg, sugar, milk, and water, a delicious beverage is prepared of considerable nutritional value. Shrub.

**Canada goldenrod.**   This plant is found in eastern North America, the seeds being a source of food. There are several related species of similar attributes. It has been recommended for use in times of scarcity as an emergency food supply.

**Sophias.**   There are several related species in western North America. The seeds are parched and ground and then made into porridge. Perennials.

**Sorghums.**   Nine major groups of sorghums

35. Canada goldenrod (*Solidago canadensis*)

exist, with various sub-species and varieties, possessing distinctive characteristics. The grains can be used for making flour. Annual grasses.

**Yam beans.**   Tropical species, grown in Africa. The seeds are edible. Perennials.

**Sand and mesa dropseeds.**   A North American species, seen in the western United States. The seeds are used as food. Perennials.

**Australian dropgrass.**   Found in Queensland. The seeds are milled into flour which, when mixed with water and baked, provides good cakes. Perennial.

**Krobonko, oyster nut.**   This species belongs to warm regions of Africa. The oily seeds are edible. Perennial vine. Another related type is Zanzibar oil vine, which also bears seeds for consumption.

**Themeda.**   The grains of this grass are used

for food. The plant is native to Australia, Africa and India.

**Wheats.**   Apart from the ordinary cultivated wheat, there is a wide choice of other wheat plants for grain production (see the table overleaf).

**Wild rice, Indian rice.**   The grains of this plant are popular and well liked. Found in eastern North America, especially southern areas. Perennial grass.

## Culture of Grains and Seeds and their Utilization

Grain and seed-bearing plants require balanced nutrition, that is to say, a mixture of adequate amounts of nitrogen, potash, phosphorus and the other essential foods. If the nitrogen level is too high, which can occur should the soil be too rich, the danger is that the plants will produce far too much straw and not enough seed. In addition, inclement weather will cause them to lie or fall down – or lodge, as this fault is called – should they be excessively gross in foliage development. It is therefore necessary to avoid too rich a soil for seed and grain growing, or great quantities of manures and fertilizers. Farmyard manure or good compost, lime as appropriate, and waste vegetation deeply buried in the ground are excellent for grain output.

If sowing seeds in gardens or fields, the seed-bed should be well tilled, but not allowed to be too loose. On the contrary, it will give the best results when it is slightly on the firm side. The amounts of seed used depend on the kind of plants grown: details can be found in agricultural and horticultural manuals.

Dry grains and seeds may well follow cleaning types of crops, such as roots and potato substitutes, in a rotation, but not normally green vegetables. It is well worthwhile intercropping grains with legumes. This reduces the general need for nitrogen. The straw supplied by lesser-known

| WHEAT | | |
|---|---|---|
| Name | Origin | Type |
| Persian wheat | Caucasus | annual |
| club wheat | Europe | annual |
| emmer | Europe, Asia | annual; spring and winter emmers |
| durum wheat | Mediterranean, south Russia | annual used for macaroni, semolina and spaghetti |
| macha | Georgia, south Russia | annual |
| einkorn | Germany, Switzerland, Italy | annual |
| kharassan wheat | Mediterranean, Ethiopia, Near East | annual |
| Polish wheat, Astrakan wheat giant rye or Jerusalem wheat | central Europe | annual used for macaroni |
| spelt | Europe | annual |
| Indian dwarf wheat | Punjab and central India | annual |
| poulard wheat | Europe, North America | annual used for macaroni |

grain and seed-yielding grass species is a useful material for feeding to livestock, providing their bedding, or turning into compost. It is also used for house roofing and mat making in many countries.

After harvest or collection, grains and seeds must be dried well. This is accomplished either by exposing the cut plants or crops to the sun in warm areas or seasons, or by artificial drying in cold regions or wet times. In the latter case, care must be taken not to damage the grain or seed by burning or overheating it. When the grain is fully dried, the process of winnowing is carried out. This means separating the seed from the chaff. Then the foodstuff can be stored in dry, well-ventilated conditions.

Most lesser-known dry grains and seeds are consumed after they have been milled or ground into flour. Milling machines can be employed where quantities involved are sizeable. In cases where only smaller amounts are produced, from home gardens or plots, or where collection from wild plants has been carried out, grinding at home is quite simple. Either a stone mill can be used, or one of the simple home grinding machines available today. These are manually or electrically operated and are quick and efficient. Home production of flour or meal for bread, cakes and biscuits or porridge presents no problems.

In certain cases, seeds have to be steeped in water or well washed to remove bitter substances and then dried, before grinding or milling. Generally, it is desirable to clean and wash all grains and seeds before milling them, otherwise dirt and discoloration will appear in the flours and meals. Do not forget to dry them again well before grinding.

Home produced flours and meals for bread

and porridge taste much better than anything you can buy in shops. They are also far more nutritious and you can be sure that they are not adulterated and have no objectionable added chemicals, such as we know shop-bought foodstuffs contain.

## Cooking

The flours and meals of the lesser-known seed and dry-grain plants may be employed as substitutes for those of ordinary wheat, rye and oats, as well as for porridge, making breakfast cereals, as semolina, or in place of other cooking materials. It is merely necessary to use the same weight of the alternative substance you select for your recipes. Excellent bread, cakes, buns, biscuits, puddings and other dishes can be produced with these kinds of ingredients.

## Preserving

Dry grains and seeds or their flours and meals are dry goods and have a long life. They should be stored in suitable containers, away from damp, and protected from insects and mites.

# Chapter 7

# FRUITS IN ABUNDANCE

Fruits are the edible and more or less succulent products of plants, consisting of the tissues and the ripened seeds. This group of foods has a wide gamut of flavours, textures and colours. Fruits are so versatile that they are appreciated in menus; moreover they supply vitamins and minerals of much importance to good health and fitness. It is possible to divide fruits according to such differences as shape, cell structure, taste or appearance. We can categorize them into classes for practical purposes as shown in the table below.

## Food Value and Choice

In general, fruits contain a high percentage of water. For example, melon types may have a water content of up to ninety-two per cent, while most other kinds have between eighty and ninety per cent. Dried fruits average twenty-five per cent water. Besides these moisture values, fruits contain sugars, a moderate amount of carbohydrate, enzymes and organic acids. They are low in fat and protein. Many types are excellent sources of

| CLASSIFICATION OF FRUITS | |
|---|---|
| *Type* | *General Use* |
| berries | in fresh fruit dishes, pies, desserts and drinks. |
| citrus (orange/lemon types) | as fresh fruit, in salads; juices as drinks |
| drupes (fleshy portion surrounding single seed) | as fresh fruit, in jams, jellies, pies and puddings |
| grapes | as fresh fruit, in jams, jellies; juice as drink |
| melons | as fresh fruit or in salads, jams |
| pomes (apple/pear types) | as fresh fruit, in pies, jams, jellies, sauces and desserts |
| miscellaneous: bananas, dates, figs, pineapples, papayas, pomegranates, avocados, etc. | as fresh fruit, in salads, ices, pies, confections and desserts; juices as drinks. |

vitamin C, and the yellow-coloured fruits contain carotene, the precursor of vitamin A. Calcium and iron may be found in various species and dried produce has a good store of the latter element. An additional contribution of fruits lies in their high cellulose content which provides much-needed roughage in our diet. This bulk material is necessary to check constipation, which is a troublesome ailment in modern industrial societies, due to the amount of processed products eaten and the badly balanced selection of foods to be found in many households.

It is unfortunate that most people eat a very limited selection of fresh or cooked fruits. We see in towns only a few species, such as oranges, apples, bananas, various berries, and a small number of other types. Thus the choice for urban dwellers is extremely narrow. But the fact is that there are dozens of excellent kinds of nutritious and tasty fruits growing throughout the world, either wild or under some form of culture or care, that are virtually unknown to the average member of the public. In tropical areas, the choice is wider, because fruits such as mangoes, pineapples, custard apples and guavas are available at various times of the year. Even so, vast quantities of good produce goes to waste in the countryside, simply because no one realizes its value and uses, except perhaps a handful of local inhabitants who cannot exploit or transport the commodities in question. It is indeed a tragedy that so many of the lesser-known fruits are neglected and permitted to rot away unpicked or unharvested, while millions of people in the world go short of food and lack adequate supplies of fruit in their diets.

When buying or picking fresh fruits, care should be taken to choose those in good condition, free from blemishes and bruises. They should also be of an appropriate size for their type and of a suitable degree of ripeness. Limp and wizened specimens are valueless. Avoid fruits that are overripe, mealy, bruised, soft or mushy, too hard, too colourless or too light in weight, have dark patches or cracked skins and look shrivelled or dull in appearance. Other bad faults are: mould, leaking of juice, sponginess, bleaching, dry skin, very soft rind, decay spots, unpleasant odour, and bloating.

## Useful Types of Fruit

Our aim here is to present to readers the names and general characteristics of various lesser-known fruit plants which yield valuable produce. Some of these have their own distinctive flavours and qualities, but many others can be employed as substitutes or alternatives for commonly consumed fruits, such as oranges, apples, lemons, bananas and so on. Many of the fruits that we buy in shops today are harvested from hybrid varieties in commercial orchards. They are frequently tasteless and of low nutritional content. Moreover, they may have been treated with poisonous sprays during the growing period or afterwards to preserve them. Naturally-grown or home-raised plants do not suffer in the same way from these disadvantages. You have only to compare the taste of your own fruits with shop-bought ones to notice the great differences. There is therefore a real need for all of us to look carefully at the merits of the vast number of lesser-known fruits and to try to search for and collect these, or else to grow at least a few of them in our gardens or backyards.

Here is a selection of fruits which should contain some types to appeal to every individual palate.

**Guabiroda.** A Brazilian species, sometimes cultivated. The fruits are orange-yellow in colour and have a flavour like that of guavas. Small tree.

**Pitahaya, naranjada.** This is a dry-area, cactus-type of small tree. It is found in Texas, Mexico and Central America, as well as the

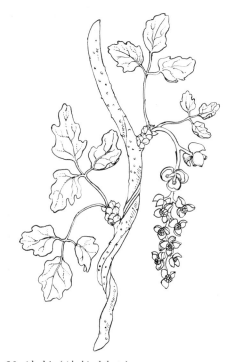

36. Akebia (*Akebia lobata*)

37. Shad bush or service berry (*Amelanchier canadensis*)

north of South America. The fruits are red in hue.

**Narasplant.** An African shrub, which bears fruits about the size of oranges, with a pleasant acid taste. They can be eaten fresh or preserved. The plants are thorny.

**Sapodilla.** This southern Mexican species may also be found in Guatemala and Honduras. It is often cultivated. The fruits are of fine quality, round to oval in shape, with a soft, sweet, yellow-brown pulp. The flavour is exotic and rich. Tree.

**Nara cherry.** Found in the southern areas of South America. Bears red fruits about the size of cherries. Shrub or small tree.

**Wild tobacco.** A shrub of warm regions of the Americas. The fruits are edible and can be made into jellies. Belongs to the family *Solanaceae*.

**Tara.** This is a plant of Manchuria, North China and eastern Siberia, also found in North Korea. The fruits resemble cherries in size though they can be as large as plums. They are much esteemed. In some places the fruits are dried for winter use and the product is called kismis. They are also baked in bread and pastry to form a kind of fruit cake. Woody vine, perennial.

**Hupeh vine.** A Chinese species, which bears edible fruits of good quality, about as large as a hen's egg. Used in preserves and for jams. Woody vine.

**Silver vine.** Another Chinese species, grows in northern areas and Manchuria. The fruits are salted in Japan. Woody vine.

**Akebia.** Found in Japan, where the fruits are often eaten and sold in markets. Woody vine.

**Hawaiian plum.** The scarlet fruits are eaten in the Hawaiian Islands. Tree.

**Saskatoon service berry**, western service berry. A North American species. The fruits are edible. Small tree.

**Shad bush, shadblow service berry, service berry.** This belongs to the area of eastern

North America. The fruits possess good flavour and are used in pies, as well as being canned for winter consumption. Small tree.

**Martin's grape.**    Native to the Philippine Islands, this species bears large bunches of dark maroon-red to black-coloured fruits. They are acid, but excellent for jellies. Woody vine.

**Dwarf almond.**    Indigenous to eastern Europe and Siberia. The fruits are eaten. Small tree.

**Brazilian cherimoyas.**    There are two species in Brazil bearing cherimoya-like fruits. Shrubs and small trees. Produce eaten locally.

**Ilama.**    Found in Central America, this plant is often cultivated. The fruits resemble cherimoyas, with a fine flavour. Small tree.

**Pond apple.**    This species grows in southern Florida and the West Indies. The fruits are somewhat insipid, but are used in jellies. Small tree.

**Wild cherimoya.**    Common in Jalisco in Mexico and bears edible fruits. These are boiled with those of other species to form sweetmeats. Shrub.

**Mann's cherimoya.**    An African species. The fruits are large and of good flavour, much eaten locally. Small tree.

**Mountain soursop, cimarrona.**    This West Indian species bears fruits with a pleasant, refreshing flavour. Small tree.

**Soncoya.**    A Central American species, sometimes cultivated. The fruits have an agreeable taste and are often sold in markets. Recommended for selective breeding to improve the strains. Small tree.

**Posh té.**    This is another Central American species, occasionally cultivated. The fruits are aromatic and of delicious taste. The flavour is richer than the ordinary soursop and the peel thicker. This plant has been recommended for selective breeding to get thinner-skinned fruits for export. Small tree.

**Anona del monte.**    This is a species of Honduras and Guatemala. It resembles posh té and is very juicy. Small tree.

The above named nine plants are of the family *Annonaceae* and related to the ordinary cherimoya, soursop (also called guanabana or corossol), custard apple or bullock's heart, sugar apple or sweet sop, and sugar apple-cherimoya hybrids, so well-known in commerce.

**Chinese laurel.**    This species is native to south-east Asia and Australia. It bears red to black berries in clusters, suitable for making jellies, syrups and brandies, as well as a sauce for eating with fish dishes. Tree.

**Hawaiian laurel.**    The fruits of this tree are pink and are eaten in jellies and syrups and used for wine production. Native of Hawaii.

**Andrachne.**    A Mediterranean species, which bears edible fruits. Shrub.

**Canary madrone.**    The berries are made into sweetmeats. Native to the Canary Islands. Shrub.

**Strawberry tree.**    Found in the Mediterranean region, this shrub produces edible berries, which are sweet in taste and mealy. They are made into preserves and wines or liqueurs.

**Manzanita.**    A western North American plant. The berries are used for jellies and making cider. Shrub. (*Illustrated overleaf.*)

**Pointleaf manzanita.**    A species of California and Mexico. The fruits are edible. Shrub.

**Bearberry.**    Grows in the northern hemisphere and withstands considerable cold. The fruits are eaten. Shrub. (*Illustrated overleaf.*)

**Chilean wineberry, macqui.**    The fruits are edible, though small, and the plant is much liked in Chile. Shrub.

**New Zealand macqui.**    Fruits eaten locally. Shrub or small tree.

**Japanese apricot.**    Indigenous to Japan and China, where it is cultivated. The fruits can be eaten raw or preserved in sugar as candies. They are also salted and boiled. There are many varieties, such as komume, tokomume, bungomume, and yatsubusa-no-mume. Small tree.

38. Manzanita (*Arctostaphylos manzanita*)

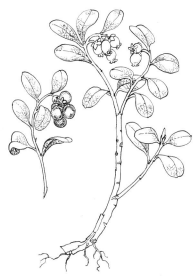

39. Bearberry (*Arctostaphylos uva-ursi*)

**Brazilian chestnuts.**   The pulp has an agreeable taste, which is similar to that of our own chestnuts. Tree.

**Dadak.**   Found in Sumatra. The fruits are as large as hens' eggs and are edible but acid. Tree. The Java dadak is very similar, but the fruits are slightly smaller, resembling plums, and are used in jellies.

**Lakoocha.**   A tropical tree, often cultivated. The fruits have a pleasant sub-acid taste and are sold in markets.

**Marang.**   This resembles the common jackfruit, so well-known in India and Malaysia. It bears round or oblong fruits, which are aromatic, sweet, juicy and of good flavour. Some people consider them superior to jackfruits. Tree.

**Champedak.**   Another south-east Asian type, this tree bears fruits which are used in soups.

**Monkey jack.**   Native to Malaysia, this species produces round-shaped fruits of pleasant flavour. Tree.

**American pawpaw.**   Native to eastern North America and found in Florida and Texas. The fruits are greenish to yellowish, of oval shape, with a sweet taste. Sometimes sold in shops and markets. Recommended for scientific breeding to improve strains. Shrub or small tree.

**Kaurie.**   Berries eaten locally in New Zealand. Large herb. Perennial.

**Astroloma.**   Two species of astrolomas occur in Australia. The fruits have sweet pulp and are much liked locally. Shrubs.

**Desert lemon.**   An Australian tree, found in New South Wales and Queensland. The fruits are consumed in jellies or as preserves. Shrub or small tree.

**Cucumber tree, bilimbi.**   This species probably came originally from Malaysia. The fruits are very acid, about 2 to 3 inches long and light yellow in colour. They are used in drinks, marmalade, jellies and syrups and may be candied or pickled. Tree. Cultivated. This species is related and similar to the well-known carambola.

**Queensland avicennia.** Fruits are baked or steamed. Tree, grows in coastal areas.

**Baccaurea.** Four species grow in south-east Asia, where their fruits are eaten raw, cooked or preserved. Trees.

**Peach palm.** A South American plant, cultivated since pre-Columbian times. The peach-like fruits are an important local food. They are eaten boiled or roasted. Tree.

**Small peach palm.** Grows in Colombia and bears edible fruits, often sold in markets. Tree.

**Crucito, tintero.** This woody plant is found from Mexico down to Panama. The fruits are eaten locally.

**Magellan barberry.** Found in southern Chile and withstands cold conditions. The fruits are often eaten locally and made into preserves. Shrub.

**Alleghany barberry.** Native to eastern North America, this species yields fruits very suitable for jellies. Also called the American barberry. Shrub.

**Barberry.** This plant grows in New Mexico and Colorado. The fruits make good jellies. Shrub.

**European barberry.** The small red berries are used in jams and preserves. A good French jam called 'Confiture d'Epine Vinette' is made from these fruits, belonging to a seedless variety. Shrub.

**Koenig akee.** The king akee, this species is found in Africa and the West Indies. Akee apples, as the fruits are called, have a nutty flavour and are firm and oily, but must be eaten quickly after picking or they may go rancid. They can be fried in butter or consumed with salted fish. Akees are cultivated in the West Indies. The fruits are about 3 inches long.

**Burmese mango-plum.** Found in the Indo-Chinese peninsula and Malaysia, this species bears edible fruits, about the size of small mangoes. Tree.

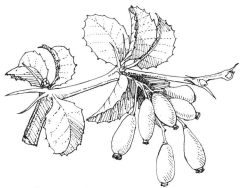

40. Barberry (*Berberis vulgaris*)

**Mango plum.** The fruits resemble a yellow plum, but have a slight mango taste. They can be consumed raw or cooked, as well as made into pickles. Tree. Found in Malaysia.

**Woolly buckthorn.** Native to the eastern parts of the United States, especially Florida. The black fruits are eaten. The Mexican buckthorn is related and its immature fruits are pickled in salt or vinegar. Shrubs or small trees.

**Bunchosia.** Grown throughout the Andes Mountains, this plant bears round fruits of greenish colour, some 1–2 inches in length, with cream or white pulp and of sweet taste. Sometimes eaten. Shrub or small tree.

**Sapote, marmalade plum, Mamey Colorado.** This species grows in Central America. The fruits are elliptic, of russet-brown coloration, and firm-fleshed with one large seed. They may be eaten raw or made into sherbets and jams. In Cuba, a substitute guava cheese is produced from sapotes and also a thick jam called 'Crema de Mamey Colorado'. Tree.

**Green sapote.** Another Central American type, which bears fruits more delicate than sapote. The pulp is pale brown, very sweet and juicy and is eaten fresh or preserved. It is much esteemed locally. Tree.

**Guabirada.** Found in southern Brazil, this plant produces fruits, about 1–1½ inches in diameter and yellow-orange in colour. Sometimes cultivated. Shrub.

**Strawberry guabirada.**   Native to Guyana and the West Indies. The fruits have a pleasant taste, the flavour resembling that of strawberries. Shrub.

**Bulungu.**   An African species, which yields violet-coloured fruits resembling plums. Tree.

**Canthium.**   A tropical African shrub or small tree. Edible fruits of excellent quality.

**Mountain papaya.**   Found in Colombia and Ecuador, this species provides fruits which are candied or preserved, but not often eaten raw. Tree. Peruvian papaya, papaya de terra fria, and higicho are very similar types of the same regions.

**Babaco, papaya de mico, and higuera del monte.**   These are related to papayas and are eaten locally in their areas of origin in Central and South America. Small trees.

**Caranda.**   A large shrub of India. The berries, about $\frac{3}{4}$ inch in diameter, are made into jellies and the ripe fruits used for pies. There is a related species in Australia which bears small, reddish-coloured fruits.

**Natal plum.**   Grows in Natal, South Africa and other parts of warm, tropical regions. The berries are bright red, about 1–2 inches in length. They may be used in pies when ripe, or when half-ripe made into jellies. Often sold in markets. Shrub.

**South Australian plum.**   The fruits are ovoid, about the size of small plums, and have a pleasant taste. They are eaten locally. Small shrub.

**Sahuaro.**   A giant cactus which grows in dry parts of the south-western United States and northern Mexico. The fruits are eaten raw, cooked, dried or preserved. They are also the source of a syrup.

**White sapote.**   Found in Mexico and Central America. The plants are sometimes cultivated. The fruits are esteemed for desserts and are about the size of oranges. They are of a yellow colour, with soft melting pulp, rather bitter-sweet, and of aromatic flavour. Often eaten fresh or used in drinks. There are several strains or unselected varieties. Tree. The Guatemalan sapote is similar in type and product.

**Common hackberry, beaver wood.**   A North American species. The Mississippi hackberry is similar. Fruits are sometimes eaten. Tree.

**Western hackberry.**   Grows in the southwest of the United States. Edible fruits. Tree.

**Sellov's hackberry.**   Found in South America. It bears edible fruits. Tree.

**Saracha.**   Native of the western United States. The berries are eaten locally. Perennial plant. Well liked by the Hopi and Navajo peoples.

**Icaco plum.**   Found in warm regions of the Americas. The fruits are eaten in preserves and jams. Shrub.

**Angolan plum.**   African species, similar to icaco plum.

**Odara pear.**   Another African species, which bears fruits of an apricot colour, much esteemed locally. It has a pleasant taste and acid pulp. Eaten largely in Nigeria. Tree.

**Antilles pear.**   Native to West Indies and produces edible fruits. Tree.

**Cainito, star-apple.**   This is another West Indian tree. It is cultivated. The fruits are about the size of apples, white to purple in colour, and hard. The pulp is of good quality and the fruit can be eaten raw or as a preserve. There are two types: cainito blanco, which is white, and cainito morado, which is purple.

**Macoucou.**   Indigenous to Guyana. The fruits are the size of pears and yellow-orange in colour. Tree.

**Magalis.**   A South African plant, which yields bright scarlet fruits, about 1 inch in diameter, with flesh of pleasant flavour. Small tree.

**Michino.**   A South American species, found in Colombia and Peru. Bears yellow fruits with whitish pulp. Tree.

**West Indian michino.** Fruits similar to gooseberries, very sweet and of pleasant taste. Tree.

**Citrus species.** Common citrus species are oranges, lemons and grapefruits. Some lesser-known citrus are given in the table below.

**Wampi.** A small tree of South China, often cultivated, with fruits the size of grapes. They have a yellow colour and a pleasant flavour. Introduced into the Americas.

**Willdenow's wampi.** Similar to wampi, but bears edible berries the size of cherries and of agreeable taste. Small tree.

**Gaudi.** A Hawaiian species, yielding sweet, yellow berries. Shrub.

**Clidemia.** Four species, the fruits of which are consumed by Mexican Indians. One type is called triana. Woody plants.

**Coccinea.** Found in tropical areas. The fruits are eaten raw, candied or cooked. Sometimes cultivated. Perennial vine.

**Sea grape.** Native of tropical America. The fruits are edible and are used for making jelly and drinks. Shrub.

**Bluewood condalia.** Grows in Texas. The fruits make a good jelly. Shrub.

**Cornelian cherry.** Native to Europe and Asia Minor. The fruits have a slightly sweet and agreeable taste. They may be eaten fresh or made into jams and marmalade. In France a beverage called *'vin de cornoulle'* is prepared from the produce of this shrub.

**Zapote Amarillo.** Indigenous to Mexico. Fruits eaten locally. Shrub.

**Couma.** A tree of Guyana, which bears fruits above the size of a guava and spherical in shape. The sweet pulp has a pleasant taste.

**Azerolier.** Grown in southern Europe and

| LESSER-KNOWN CITRUS FRUITS | |
| --- | --- |
| *Name* | *Use* |
| hystrix | bears lemon-scented fruits and is found in the Philippines |
| sweet lemon | fruits yellow and sweet |
| Nimeng or Canton lemon, otalite orange, khatta tanaka or khatta orange | similar to ordinary lemon |
| tamisan | very juicy fruits, good flavour, mildly acid, a pleasant breakfast food |
| musk lime | very small orange with musky fragrance |
| blanco or calamondin | looks like a small tangerine, very acid; used in drinks, tea, marmalade and jellies |
| king orange | similar to ordinary orange, coarse-peeled |
| Webb's orange | fruits used like ordinary lemons |

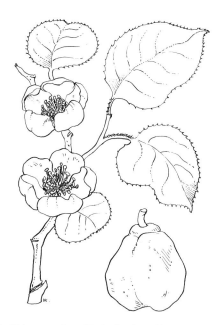

41. Manzanilla (*Crataegus stipulosa* or *mexicana*)

42. Chinese quince (*Cydonia sinensis*)

North Africa. The fruits may be eaten fresh or preserved. There are varieties with yellow, red and white colouring. Shrub or small tree.

**Black haw.**    Indigenous to the Pacific coastal region of North America. The fruits are juicy and sweet and are used in making jellies. Tree.

**Summer haw.**    Found in the southern United States. The fruits are somewhat pear-shaped and of yellowish-colour. Esteemed for making jellies. Small tree.

**Hupeh haw.**    A Chinese species, bears scarlet fruits, 1 inch long. Fruits are liked locally. Often cultivated. Tree.

**Mexican hawthorn.**    Fruits are used locally in preserves and jellies. Tree.

**American hawthorn.**    Native to central United States. Fruits used in jellies. Tree.

**May hawthorn.**    European species, grows in cooler regions. The fruits can be dried and ground into flour for addition to bread. Tree.

**Chinese haw.**    Found in northern China and Siberia. Often cultivated. The fruits are eaten

stewed, candied, preserved, in jelly or as sweetmeats. Often sold in Chinese markets. Tree.

**Manzanilla.**    This species grows from Guatemala to Ecuador. Often cultivated. The fruits are mealy, have a pleasant flavour and may be stewed or made into syrup. Sold in local markets.

**Cudrania.**    Two species found in eastern Asia and down to Australia. Fruits are eaten fresh or preserved. Perennials.

**Persoon or quince.**    Found in temperate regions of Europe, Asia and North America. The fruits are pear or apple-shaped and are used in jams and marmalades. Small tree.

**Chinese quince.**    Bears very large fruits, made into sweetmeats. Often cultivated. Tree.

**Persimmon types.**    A large number of plants belong to *Diospyros* species. All types are trees. Some of those yielding fruits for consumption are given in the table opposite.

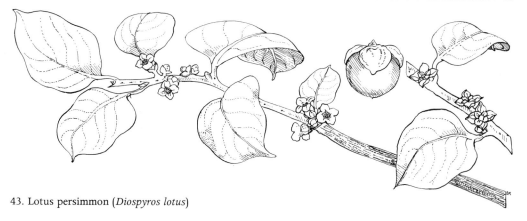

43. Lotus persimmon (*Diospyros lotus*)

| | PERSIMMON TYPES | |
|---|---|---|
| *Name* | *Product* | *Origin* |
| brown ebony | edible fruit | Cameroons |
| oaxaca plum | edible fruit, with fine flavour | Mexico |
| mabolo or butter fruit | fruit roundish, velvety, with dry flesh of a dark cream colour | Malaysia and Philippines |
| black sapote (zapote negro) | fruits with blackish pulp eaten fresh; orange or lemon juice added when eaten; cultivated | Mexico |
| timbiri | fruits edible, but astringent | tropical Asia and Africa |
| kaki or Japanese persimmon | fruits have the size and appearance of tomatoes and are red to orange in colour; pulp is the same hue, can be eaten raw, or sometimes dried; numerous varieties, including fuyuaki, hackiya, tamopan, tsuru and tanenashi | China, Japan, Mediterranean areas, southern United States |
| lotus persimmon | fruits eaten fresh, dried or overripe; cultivated | West Asia and China |
| Zanzibar ebony, West African ebony or swamp ebony | pulp of fruit made into a fermented drink, or used for making soft toffee called *ma'di* | tropical Africa |
| common persimmon | fruits are edible, but variable in quality; several varieties | eastern North America to Florida and Texas |

**Tamarind plum.** A Malaysian species, which bears small, black fruits, esteemed as delicacies. Tree.

**Maingayi.** Similar to the tamarind plum. There are two other related species in Malaysia.

**Dillenia.** There are four species in the Philippine Islands. The fruits are used for jams and sauces. Trees.

**Cunningham plum.** An Australian species, found especially in Queensland. The fruits are edible, with orange-red arillus (seed case or covering) and sweet, sub-acid taste and pleasant flavour. Used for preserves. Small tree.

**Chirimote.** Native of Ecuador, bearing tender, crisp and juicy fruits. Sometimes sold in local markets. Shrub.

**Popenoei.** Similar to chirimote. Shrub.

**Kei apple, umkokolo.** This species is native to South Africa. It bears globose fruits, shaped like small apples, about $1-1\frac{1}{2}$ inches in diameter, and of greenish-yellow colour. The pulp is juicy, aromatic and acid. Kei apples are used for jams, compote and marmalades. The unripe fruits can be made into jellies. Small tree.

**Ketembilla, Ceylon gooseberry.** A small, spiny tree or shrub, native to tropical Asia, but introduced into warmer regions in other parts of the world. The berries are $\frac{3}{4}-1$ inch in diameter and are dark purple to black in colour. In texture they are velvety and full of juice, resembling a gooseberry. Recommended for jellies and jams, also served as sauce with meat and fish.

**Pitahaya de agosto.** Grows in dry areas of northern Mexico and Texas. The fruits are edible and measure 1–2 inches across. The colour is purplish. Shrub.

**Strawberry cactus.** Another American dry-area species. The fruits have a delicious strawberry taste and can be eaten raw or in preserves. Shrub.

**Mexican strawberry, pitahaya.** This plant bears pleasant-tasting fruits. It is indigenous to west Texas and New Mexico. Shrub.

**Nepal elaeagnus.** Fruits eaten locally. Found in tropical Asia. Shrub.

**Cherry elaeagnus.** A Japanese tree, which bears fruits used for jam-making or in beverages.

**Philippine elaeagnus.** The fruits are made into a very fine jelly. They are pink to pale red in colour, sub-acid to sour and measure up to 1 inch in diameter. Shrub.

**Japanese elaeagnus.** The fruits are eaten after scalding. Shrub.

**New Zealand damson.** The fruit resembles a common damson and is much esteemed locally. Tree.

**Amboina berry.** Found in Java and East Indies. The red berries are up to 2 inches long. Fruits may be eaten raw or cooked. Shrub.

**Wild olive.** Native to East Bengal, northeastern Himalaya Mountains and Malaysia. The fruits are used in curry dishes or pickled in the same way as olives locally. Tree.

**Manzanilla.** A species of Ecuador, which bears light red, globose fruits. These are soft and juicy and have the flavour of pears. Shrub.

**Yucatan chestnut.** Young fruits are eaten locally in south Mexico. Tree.

**Erioglossum.** The fruits are edible, roundish-oblong in shape and about $\frac{3}{4}$ inch in diameter. Native to tropical Asia. Small tree.

**Chiotilla.** A plant of dry areas. Native to Mexico. The fruit is sometimes sold in local markets. Cactus type.

**Soroco.** A small tree suited to dry regions. Found in Ecuador and Peru. The fruits are sweet and edible.

**Santal Fruit.** An Australian species, which bears fleshy fruits that can be eaten raw or made into jam. The seeds are also edible. Shrub.

**Eugenias.** There are many useful species, listed in the table opposite, which all belong to the myrtle family. Trees or shrubs.

| Name | EUGENIAS<br>Product | Origin |
|------|---------------------|--------|
| watery rose-apple | red fruits, rather insipid, often eaten raw or made into a syrup called *roedjak*; sold in Java; cultivated | Malaysia, Sri Lanka, Indonesia |
| Conzatt's rose-apple | fruits eaten locally | South Mexico |
| lipoti | fruits have a pleasant taste and acid flavour, are dark red to black and about $\frac{3}{4}$ inch in diameter; eaten raw, made into wine and an excellent jelly; sometimes cultivated | Philippines |
| Java jambosa | edible fruits of fair quality | Java and Malaysia |
| grumichama | fruits are small and dark crimson in hue, with variations in quality; they have a pleasant flavour when raw and make good jams, jellies and pies; sometimes cultivated | Peru and southern Brazil |
| vinegar jambosa | edible fruits, sold in markets and used for making vinegar | Argentine and Brazil |
| rumberry or murta | fruits are dark red to black and are made into a liqueur or jam | West Indies |
| arrayan | bears dark purple fruits of delicate texture, with whitish, juicy pulp, sub-acid and of pleasant taste; eaten raw | Ecuador |
| Formosa jambosa | fruits small and round, rather insipid; sold in local markets and cultivated in Vietnam | tropical Asia |
| Java plum or jambolan | fruits are small and purple in colour and are made into jams; some varieties are seedless; good taste | tropical Asia to Australia |
| rose apple or jambos | reddish fruits, which are juicy and crisp, with a sweet taste; used for jellies with the addition of some other acid fruit and in sauces; may also be candied; cultivated | tropics of Asia and Africa; also introduced to the Americas |
| mankil or samarang rose apple | ovoid, edible fruits of good flavour, red, fleshy and acid, about $2\frac{1}{2}$ inches long; much eaten in Java | Malaysia, Indonesia and Philippines |
| pera do campo | pear-shaped fruits which are juicy, acid and very aromatic; used for jellies; occasionally cultivated | central Brazil |

| | | |
|---|---|---|
| pitomba | the broadly ovate, yellow-orange fruits are juicy and aromatic and are made into jellies; sometimes cultivated | Brazil, especially Bahia |
| mountain apple | There are several varieties of these fruits, which are of red colour; cultivated | tropical Asia |
| bush cherry or red myrtle | fruits are made into jellies | Australia, especially New South Wales and Queensland |
| Borneo jambosa | edible fruits, suitable for jellies; much esteemed locally; recommended for scientific breeding; cultivated | Borneo and India |
| maigang | fruits are about $\frac{3}{4}$ inch broad and of dark red colour, acid and can be made into an excellent tart jelly | Philippine Islands |
| pitanga tuba | fruits are ribbed and aromatic, acid; very suitable for jam | Brazil |
| cabelluda | fruits resemble gooseberries and are juicy with a pleasant sub-acid taste; suitable for jellies | Brazil |
| surinam cherry or pitanga | fruits the size of cherries, but ribbed and orange to orange-red in colour, shading to almost black, of aromatic flavour; can be eaten raw, in jams, jellies, compote, sherbet, syrup and tarts; much esteemed locally; cultivated | tropical and sub-tropical Americas |
| uvalha | fruits are yellow to orange in colour, with pleasant aroma; they have a high juice-content and are used for drinks | southern Brazil |

**Feijoa.** Common in the southern parts of South America, where it is cultivated. Feijoa fruits are eaten raw or stewed and have a pleasant flavour. They are also made into jams and jellies. There is much variation between individual trees, as far as fruit taste goes.

**Leon lemon.** Dry-area species of northern Mexico and Texas. The fruits are used in cooking as a substitute for lemons. Cactus type.

**Elephant apple, wood apple.** This plant bears edible fruit, the size of an orange, with rather glutinous aromatic pulp. It can be eaten raw, in jellies and sherbets, and is considered stimulating and good for the stomach. Small tree. Indigenous to India and Sri Lanka.

| FIG TYPES | | |
| Name | Product | Origin |
| --- | --- | --- |
| rough-leaved fig, noomaie, balemo | black fruits, eaten locally | Australia, especially Victoria and Queensland |
| Cape fig | fruits eaten locally | South Africa |
| East African fig | fruits are succulent and edible | East Africa |
| Mexican fig | fruits consumed locally | Mexico and Central America |
| okgue | fruits made into jellies | Japan, Taiwan and China |
| peepul or bot tree | sacred to Hindus and Buddhists; small fruits used as famine food | tropical Asia |
| Roxburgh fig | bears large fruits consumed locally, as big as ordinary common figs | Indo-China and India |
| Bali fig | fruits eaten locally | Malaysia and Indonesia |
| Madagascar fig | fruits are about 3 inches long and slightly aromatic, pear-shaped or roundish, and yellow to red in colour; sweet in taste like common figs; eaten raw or in preserves | Madagascar |
| Sycomore fig | slightly aromatic fruits; cultivated | North Africa |
| dye fig | fruits eaten locally | Polynesia |
| Angolan fig | ripe fruits consumed locally | tropical Africa |

**Fig types.**   Numerous kinds of *Ficus* species provide fruits. A selection is given in the table above.

**Runeala plum.**   A species native to India and Malaysia but introduced into the Americas. The fruits are round, about $\frac{3}{4}$ inch wide and of russet-purple colour, with creamy white pulp. They are slightly acid and have a pleasant taste. Much used for compotes. Shrub.

**Mindanao plum.**   Indigenous to the Philippines, this shrub bears fruits some $\frac{3}{4}$ inch broad, roundish in shape, of dark purple colour and sub-acid. Recommended for jellies.

**Martinique cherry.**   Origin uncertain but probably West Indian. The berries are a brilliant red, small as cherries and slightly acid. They are suitable for jellies, but generally need sweetening if eaten fresh. There are certain varieties, however, that bear sweet fruits. Small tree.

**Botoko plum, governor's plum, ramontschi.**   It can be found in Malaysia and Madagascar, as well as being cultivated throughout the tropics. The fruits are round, about $1\frac{1}{4}$ inches long and acid. The colour is dark purple to black. They are much used in jams and preserves, but are also eaten with fish in a sauce. Shrub.

**Rukam.**   A species of Malaysia and the Philippines. The fruits are round and dark red. It is cultivated. May be eaten raw, if a sweeter variety is selected, especially rukum. Tree.

**Separy.**   A species of tropical Asia, grown in

Indo-China and Malaysia. The fruits are round, of dark purple hue, sweet and mildly acid. They possess a lot of juice and are eaten in pies. Shrub.

**Meiwa kumquat.** Found in China and Japan, this tree bears round orange-like fruits of sweet taste, often eaten raw. Sometimes cultivated.

**Nagami kumquat.** A Japanese plant, bearing oval, orange-type fruits. They are acid and are used in jellies, preserves and jams. Cultivated in various areas. Small tree.

**Marumi kumquat.** Another species of Japan, which produces round, acid, orange-type fruits. Used for jams, jellies and preserves. Commercially cultivated. Small tree.

**Chiloe strawberry.** This plant is cultivated in the Andes region and also occurs in the Pacific regions of North and South America. The fruits are sold in local markets. Perennial.

**Virginian strawberry.** Found in eastern North America down to Texas. The fruits are red, sometimes white, with juicy pulp and of pleasant taste. Perennial.

**Griffith's camboge.** Found in Assam and Malaysia and sometimes cultivated. Bears large yellow fruits, with acid pulp, which need much added sugar when eaten raw. They make excellent jelly and compote, and can also be cut into pieces and made into a good soup. Tree.

**Bancana.** A Malaysian species, which bears fruits eaten locally. Small tree.

**Bentham's bancana.** An Indo-Chinese and Malayan species, producing edible fruits with white pulp of pleasant flavour. Small tree.

**Binucao.** This is an eastern Indian species, also found in Malaysia, Indonesia and the Philippine Islands. The fruits are lemon-yellow in colour, rather flattened and about $1\frac{1}{2}$–2 inches in diameter with acid pulp. Often eaten with fish dishes, Small tree.

**Mundu.** The fruits are yellow to orange in hue and are eaten locally. Sometimes cultivated. They are sub-acid and may be made into jam. Found in south-east Asia. Tree.

**Goraka, Cambodian gamboge.** Bears edible fruits of a pleasant taste. Tree.

**Nicobar gamboge.** This species is indigenous to the Nicobar Islands and Malaya. The fruits taste like peaches and are of fine quality. The plant has been recommended for improvement and commercial use by selective breeding. Tree.

**Bridonnes.** A species of tropical Asia, often cultivated. The fruits have a pleasant acid flavour, not unlike mangostans (see below), and can be eaten raw or made into jellies and syrup. Tree.

**Mangostan or Mangosteen.** A small tree of the Molucca Islands. Cultivated all over the tropics. It is an outstanding dessert fruit, The berries are round, about the size of a tangerine, with thick, smooth rind of red-purple colour. The pulp resembles that of a well-ripened plum. Mangostans may be seedless or have up to three seeds in the fruits. The pulp may be cooked with rice (*lempog*) or with syrup (*dodol*) for culinary usage.

**Black gamboge.** A Malayan tree which bears oval fruits, up to $1\frac{1}{2}$ inches in length, of orange colour and possessing a sweet and agreeable pulp. They are eaten locally.

**Small-leaved gamboge.** Another Malaysian species, yielding small, cherry-sized fruits of yellow colour. Eaten locally with hot peppers, fish and soya to form an appetizing dish. Small tree.

**Planchoni.** A species of Vietnam and adjacent countries. The fruits are up to 3 inches long, of yellow-green colour and have a sub-acid pulp. The taste is agreeable. Also eaten dried. Tree.

**Prainiana.** A Malaysian tree bearing fruits with sub-acid flavour.

**Bengal gamboge.** Fruits consumed fresh locally. Also found in Malaysia and the Philippines. Tree.

**Egg tree.** The yellow fruits produced by this species, native to India and Malaya, are

44. Virginian strawberry (*Fragaria virginiana*)

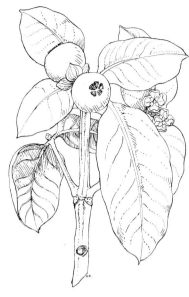

45. Mangosteen (*Garcinia mangostana*)

about the size of a small orange with a pointed projection at one end. The yellow, juicy pulp has an acid and pleasantly refreshing flavour. Tree.

**Tasmanian gaultheria.**   Found in Tasmania and New Zealand. Edible fruits of good flavour. Shrub.

**Australian Gaultheria.**   Native to Australia, where the fruits are eaten locally. Shrub.

**Myrsinites.**   A western North American shrub, which furnishes fruits used in preserves.

**Shallon.**   Found on the North American Pacific coast from British Columbia to California. The dried fruits are eaten during winter periods and are much esteemed. Shrub.

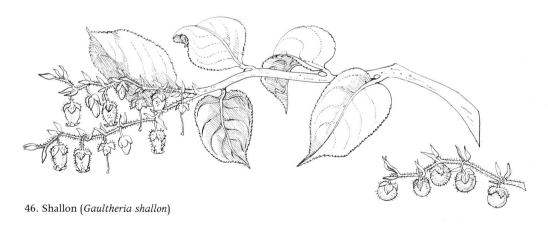

46. Shallon (*Gaultheria shallon*)

**Black huckleberry.**  Indigenous to eastern North America, this plant provides edible fruits used in pies and eaten raw. There are large-fruited improved varieties. In addition, the bear huckleberry, the dwarf huckleberry, the box huckleberry and the dangleberry are also eaten. Shrubs.

**Marmalade box or genipa.**  This is a popular fruit in Brazil and Puerto Rico. Genipas are about the size of oranges, of round shape and russet-brown in colour. The pulp is brownish and the taste pronounced. It is necessary to soften the fruits after picking before they can be eaten. A cooling drink called *'Genipapado'* is made from the fruits. Tree.

**Umari.**  These fruits are used as food in parts of Brazil. Tree.

**Gnemon.**  A species of tropical Asia. The fruits are cooked or roasted in the Philippine Islands. There is a related Indian species. Woody plant.

**Chupones.**  A native of Chile, this plant produces edible berries. Perennial.

**Anchovy pear.**  A West Indian tree, bearing brown fruits similar to mangoes in taste.

**Jamaica or red sorrel.**  The fruit capsules make good jelly, considered to be equal to red currant. White sorrel is another form of this fruit. Annual shrubs; *Hibiscus* species.

**Mangabeira.**  The fruits are ovoid in shape and about the size of plums. They have a yellow colouring mixed with red and are used for making marmalade in many areas of Brazil. Small tree.

**Haronga.**  A species of Madagascar. Bears edible fruits. Shrub.

**Kaffir Plum.**  Native to South Africa, this species bears red fruits, about 1 inch in diameter, with acid, juicy pulp. They are made into a much esteemed jelly. Tree.

**Bush apple.**  The fruit is yellow to red in colour and of pleasant flavour. The species is native to West Africa. Tree.

**Sea buckthorn.**  A species of Europe and

47. Sea buckthorn (*Hippophae rhamnoides*)

Asian temperate regions. The berries are sometimes made into jelly. They are also eaten with milk and cheese in Siberia or made into a sauce in France for accompanying meat and fish dishes. Tree.

**Japanese raisin tree.**  A tree of the Himalayan region, China and Japan. The fruits are dry and reddish-brown in colour, also sweet and sub-acid. They are much esteemed in some parts of China and Japan.

**Pitahaya oregona.**  A dry-area shrub, often cultivated in Mexico and Central America for its fruits. These are up to 5 inches in length and of excellent quality.

**Ingas.**  There are a number of these species, suited to tropical areas, which bear edible pods containing generally sweet pulp. Trees.

**Papaya oregona.**  A tree of Mexico and Central America, the fruit of which can be eaten cooked, in salads, or made into sweetmeat.

**Jarilla.**  A Mexican species, the fruits of which are used for preserves and sweetmeats. Small shrub.

48. Japanese raisin tree (*Hovenia dulcis*)

**Utah juniper.** A western North American tree, the fresh and ground dried fruits of which are eaten locally, sometimes pressed into cakes.

**Karatas.** Native to the West Indies, this bears edible fruits of pleasant taste. Perennial.

**Langsat, langseh, Duku.** This species is native to Malaysia. It bears clusters of closely-packed berries, with tough skins of a pale yellow colour. The pulp is whitish, juicy and aromatic and the fruits are useful for dessert purposes. Tree.

**Aquiboquil.** Native to Chile and Peru, the fruits possess sweet pulp and have a pleasant flavour. Sold in the local markets. Woody plant.

**Native currant.** A Tasmanian and south-eastern Australian species, which bears berries of sub-acid flavour. They are used for jellies and preserves. Woody plant.

**Sansapote or zapote cabillo.** The fruits of this Central and South American species are up to 6 inches long, with rough skins and brownish colour. In British Honduras it is called monkey apple. Often sold in local markets. Tree.

**Cina, cabesa de viejo.** A dry area species of Sonora and Baja California. Bears edible fruits. Tree.

**Argua.** Native to Colombia. The fruits are pear-shaped and yellow in colour. Much esteemed locally. Tree.

**Molina.** Found in Chile and Peru, the fruits are roundish, about the size of an apple and have to be eaten when very ripe. They have an excellent taste. Often sold in local markets. Tree.

**Caimito, abui.** The fruits are popular, especially in Brazil. Tree.

**Lucmo.** Another South American species, which bears round to oval fruits, with yellow pulp. They are mealy and should be kept in straw for a few days before being eaten. Small tree.

**Macarandiba.** Popular in Brazil, where it is a much esteemed dessert fruit. It can also be eaten preserved. Tree.

**Canistel.** The fruits of this Central American tree are ovoid and of good flavour, the colour being bright orange with mealy soft pulp. May be eaten fresh or in custards and sherbets. The plant is also a source of spice. Tree.

**Yellow sapote, zapote amarillo.** This species bears edible fruits. They may be eaten raw and are sold in the local markets of Panama and Costa Rica. Small tree.

**Marmalade fruit, grosse sapote, mammey sapote.** The fruits are ovoid, about 3–5 inches in length and possess sweet, reddish-tinted pulp. Found in Central America. Tree.

**Mexican sapodilla.** The fruits are smooth-skinned and yellow when ripe. Tree.

**Green sapote, injerto, yashtel.** Found in the highlands of Guatemala, this bears a fruit similar to the Mexican sapodilla. Tree.

**Mammey apple, St Domingo apricot.**
This species is found in the West Indies
and Central America. The fruit is nearly
spherical, with thick, brown, bark-like skin.
Small tree.

**Calabura.**    Another tropical American species, which produces small, yellow berries for
making into jam or using in pies. Small tree.

**Honey berry, ginep, Spanish lime,
mamoncillo.**    The fruits are small, ovoid
and green in colour, with a sweetish, aromatic
taste. Well liked in Cuba and Puerto Rico.
Tree.

**Bojeri.**    The fruits are the size of small plums
and have a sweetish flavour. A tropical
American species. Tree.

**Anderson wolfberry.**    Indigenous to Arizona and California. The berries are eaten fresh
or dried and sometimes used in soups. Shrub.

**Arabian wolfberry.**    Similar to the Anderson wolfberry, but grows in North Africa.
Shrub.

**Chinese wolfberry.**    A small shrub-like
vine, native to eastern Asia.

**Popenoei, joyapa.**    This species bears globose fruits of purplish-black colour with juicy
pulp and a sweet, agreeable taste. Eaten in
Ecuador. Shrub.

**Barbados cherry.**    A species of the West
Indies and south Texas, which produces scarlet
fruits containing juicy pulp, which are used in
jellies and preserves. Shrub.

**West Indian cherry.**    Bears red fruits, similar to Barbados cherry. Tree.

**Grosse cerise de Martinique.**    Found in
tropical America and the West Indies, this
species has reddish fruits with a refreshing
taste and juicy pulp. Like the two cherries
described above, it has a good vitamin C
content.

**Mango types.**    Various species produce
fruits with mango-like attributes. Some examples are given in the table below.

**Matisia, sapote.**    This species produces
edible fruits, of brownish-green colour, with
leathery skin, but the pulp is orange-yellow,
sweet and of pleasant taste. Tree. A South
American species.

| MANGO TYPES | | |
|---|---|---|
| *Name* | *Product* | *Origin* |
| paho, or pahutan mango | fruits about 2–3½ inches long, green to yellow in colour, smooth skinned; used for pickling | Philippines |
| binjai mango | fruits eaten preserved | Malaya |
| bachang mango | acid fruit must be steeped in lime water or syrup before eating; may be made into dish called 'sambal' with hot peppers, soya and fish | Malaysia, Java |
| monjet mango | fruits eaten when ripe and fresh | Malaya |
| kurwini mango | fruits consumed when ripe and are noted for good flavour | Malaya |
| Rumph's mango | fruits used when ripe as fresh dessert and also made into preserves | Malaya |
| Ceylon mango | fruits eaten in some parts of Ceylon | Ceylon (Sri Lanka) |

**Merangara.** The fruits are eaten in Australia. Tree.

**Karkalia.** Fruits eaten raw in Australia. Also found in the south west of South America. Perennial.

**Gooseberry fig.** Related to karkalia, this plant bears fruits about the size of gooseberries. Some people find them rather insipid. Seen in South Africa and the Mediterranean region. Perennial.

**Chilean fig.** Fruits eaten locally. Small shrub.

**Hottentot fig.** A South African plant, bearing edible fruits. Eaten in Cape Province. Perennial.

**Queensland wild lime, Russell River lime.** May be used as substitute for ordinary lime. Shrub. An Australian plant.

**Ceriman.** A creeper, native to Mexico, which bears cone-like fruits, some 7–9 inches long, rather juiceless, but having a pleasant pineapple-like flavour. However, the presence of spicules of calcium oxalate in the pulp causes itching of the throat and tongue, so straining is necessary before using the pulp in ices and drinks.

**Spach's plum.** A West Indian plant, bearing small fruits about the size of plums. The taste is pleasant. Small tree. A similar species exists in Brazil, called pusa, which bears a black fruit, sold in the markets.

**Australian gooseberry.** A small, climbing shrub, the white berries of which resemble gooseberries and are used in pies, puddings and confectionary in Australia.

**Capulin.** A tropical American tree which bears sweet, red or pale yellow fruits of good flavour.

**Jaboticaba.** A Brazilian tree, the fruits of which are highly esteemed. They may be eaten raw or made into jellies. Often sold in markets. They are small and round, dark purple in colour and crowned with a disc. There are three other related species which produce similar fruits. Trees.

**Rambutan.** There are many varieties of this species, which produce dessert fruits. Cultivated in tropical Asia. Small tree.

**Longan, longyen, lengkeng.** A popular Chinese fruit, which can be eaten raw, preserved or dried. Cultivated. Tree.

**Pulasan.** This species is indigenous to Indonesia, but is much grown in China. A very popular oriental fruit. It may be eaten fresh or as a compote. The best varieties are sweet, juicy and sub-acid. Tree.

**Prickly pear.** A desert cactus. Edible fruit.

**Onkob.** A small, deciduous tree of Arabia and tropical Africa, which bears edible fruits.

**Mauritius olive.** Edible fruits, may be used in place of olives. Small tree.

**Ogeche, sour tupelo, tupelo gum, ogeeche lime.** The fruits are eaten preserved. It is a species native to South Carolina and Florida. Tree.

**Emu apple, bulloo.** An Australian species, the reddish fruits of which possess a refreshing pulp, eaten in some parts of the country. Tree.

**Otophora.** East Indian species, with orange-brown or dark purple fruits, eaten locally. Trees and shrubs.

**Guiana plum.** Bears edible fruits of good flavour. Tree.

**Curatella plum.** A tropical African species, producing well liked fruits. Tree.

**Gingerbread plum.** Edible fruits, locally esteemed. Tree. Native to warm regions of Africa.

**Mobola plum.** Bears edible fruits with a strawberry taste. One of the best wild species in South Africa. Tree.

**Nonda.** An Australian tree, with fleshy fruits (drupes) which are eaten locally.

**Candle tree.** A tropical American species, the fruits of which may be cooked or eaten raw. Tree.

**Grenadilla types.** These are vines which bear various kinds of fruits similar to passion fruit. See the table overleaf for a selection of useful grenadillas.

| | GRENADILLA TYPES | |
|---|---|---|
| *Name* | *Product* | *Origin* |
| apricot vine, May pop | fruit formerly cultivated in Virginia; made into jelly and sherbet | eastern North America |
| water-lemon, bell-apple, Jamaica honeysuckle | fruits cultivated in some areas | tropical Americas, West Indies |
| sweet grenadilla | fruits have sweet, pleasant flavour, often used at breakfast | tropical Americas |
| curuba | edible fruits; sometimes cultivated | tropical Americas |
| tasco, curuba de castilla | fruits eaten raw or in drinks, ice creams and sherbets, also made into *creme de caruba*; cultivated | Ecuador and Colombia |
| grenadille de quito | fruits of delicious fragrance | Ecuador |
| gullan | similar to tasco (*see above*) | Ecuador |
| giant grenadilla, barbardine, grenadilla real | fruits are 6–8 inches long, oval, smooth and of yellow colour; the pulp is very palatable and may be eaten raw, with wine, as a drink or in a sauce; widely cultivated | tropical America |
| long tasco | fruit oblong, about 6 inches long, deep yellow to red in colour, with juicy pulp | Ecuador |

**West Indian gooseberry, Barbados gooseberry, lemon vine.** This plant bears fruits that can be eaten raw or cooked. Woody vine.
**Selloum.** A Brazilian shrub, producing edible fruits used in compote.
**Otaheite gooseberry.** A tree of tropical India and Malaya. The fruits are $\frac{3}{4}$ to just over 1 inch long, green in colour and fairly round. They are used in preserves and pickles.
**Emblic, myrobolan.** This species is native to tropical Asia. The fruits are very acid, but make good preserves and jellies. Shrub.
**Plectronia plum.** A South African tree, which bears fruits the size of plums, light brown in colour. Considered one of the best of local native fruits.

**Queensland spiny plum.** Bears fruits the size of plums, which are used in preserves. Tree.
**Ground lemon, common May apple.** Native to eastern North America. The fruits have an agreeable taste, but must be eaten moderately because too many can cause colic. Perennial.
**Pometia.** A Polynesian species, which produces roundish and smooth, juicy edible fruits, about 2 inches in diameter, with a sweet, aromatic flavour. Tree.
**Plum and cherry types.** A considerable number of these *Prunus* species provide substitutes for common garden plums and cherries. A short list of useful trees and shrubs is given opposite.

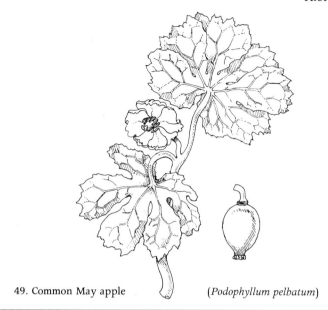

49. Common May apple        (*Podophyllum pelbatum*)

PLUM AND CHERRY TYPES

| Name | Product | Origin |
|---|---|---|
| American wild plum or river plum | fruits eaten raw or preserved; cultivated in some parts of Canada, and sold in markets; varieties include Itasca, Aitkin, Oxford, Crimson and Cheney | eastern North America as well as Florida, Texas and New Mexico, in hilly regions and Rocky Mountains areas |
| Chickasaw plum or mountain cherry* | fruits are eaten in jellies and preserves; sometimes cultivated, varieties include Ogeeche and Caddo Chief | eastern North America from Delaware to Florida and Mississippi |
| western sand cherry | fruits are of purple-black colour and sweet to taste | western North America |
| Chinese sour cherry | fruits used in preserves; cultivated in some areas | Yangtze valley of China |
| capulin | fruits are eaten raw, stewed or preserved or the juice mixed with meal to make cakes called *cupultamal*; a cherry water is prepared from the distilled leaves of the trees | found from Mexico to Peru |

* Illustrated on page 94.

| | | |
|---|---|---|
| cherry plum* | fruits are about $\frac{3}{4}$–$1\frac{1}{2}$ inches in diameter and of subglobose type | western Asia |
| sour cherry* | A temperate-zone type, often cultivated; fruits used in pies, puddings, for jams and jellies, cherry cider, glacé fruits, brandies and liqueurs | western Asia, but introduced into other regions |
| Gray's chokeberry | the young fruits, which have a pungent taste, are eaten in Japan | north Japan and west China |
| hortulana plum | used in jams and marmalades; cultivated varieties are Kanawha, Golden Beauty, Leptune, Moreman, Cumberland | central and southern United States |
| beach plum | fruits, sold in local markets, are made into jelly and jams | found from New Brunswick to Maine in North America |
| Rocky Mountain cherry | fruits made into jelly and jams | western North America |
| wild goose plum | used for jellies, jams and preserves; varieties include Osage, Texas Belle, Newman, Milton and Wildgoose | North America |
| European bird cherry* | black fruits suitable for jam | Europe, temperate Asia |
| Chinese or Japanese plum | fruits eaten fresh or cooked; varieties include Red June, Satsuma, Kelsey and Abundance | Japan, China and California |
| wild black cherry or rum cherry† | fruits used in liqueurs or for cough syrup | North America |
| apricot plum | fruits are variable in taste, sometimes resembling the flavour of almonds | North China |
| blackthorn or sloe† | fruits are blue-black in colour, with a bloom; often used for liqueurs | Europe and the Mediterranean region |
| klamath or Pacific plum | fruits eaten fresh or preserved; grow wild in large amounts and are collected locally | from Oregon to California |
| Manchu cherry | sweet and juicy fruits | Japan |
| hog plum or black sloe | fruits popular for jelly and jam | eastern coastal plain of North America |
| common choke cherry | fruits used in pies and jellies; sometimes sold in local markets | North America |

---

* *Illustrated on page 94.*      † *Illustrated on page 95.*

**Apple and pear types.**   Several *Pyrus* species are found wild or yield useful lesser-known fruits. A selection is given below.

**Randia.**   A species of tropical Asia, bearing yellow fruits, which are eaten cooked. There is another species in the warm regions of the Americas, the fruits of which yield an edible pulp. Small trees.

**Reptonia.**   A small tree of eastern India. The fruits are drupes, sweet in taste and much esteemed locally. Sold in markets.

**Darling plum, red ironwood.**   A species indigenous to the Bahama Islands and southern Florida. The fruits are purple to black in colour and of pleasant taste. Shrub.

**Bakupari.**   The fruits are ovate and of orange-yellow hue, with tough skins. The flesh is sub-acid and white. Used in jams and much liked locally. A native plant of Brazil. Tree.

**Limao do matto.**   A species of tropical America, that bears yellowish fruits of good taste which are utilized for jam making. Sometimes cultivated especially in Brazil. Small tree.

**Bacuru pary.**   Another Brazilian species,

## APPLE AND PEAR TYPES

| Name | Product | Origin |
| --- | --- | --- |
| crab apple | fruits used for making jellies, jam, pickles, preserves and cider or vinegar | eastern North America northern Europe |
| northern Chinese crab apple* | fruits eaten fresh, dried or preserved | north China, Siberia and Manchuria |
| Chinese pear | fruits eaten raw or with game or meat; there are a number of varieties, such as Yakwamli, Peking Pear, Paili, Peisooli, Ta Suan Li | China |
| fragrant crap or crab* | used in same way as crab apple | eastern North America |
| southern Chinese crab apple* | fruits used for jellies and preserves; leaves as tea substitute | China and north-east India, especially Assam |
| Chinese apple | fruits eaten fresh or in preserves; Paipingkua is a white apple from Peking and Hongtengku is a red apple from Pautingfu | eastern temperate regions of China |
| ringo apple | fruits eaten in Japan after slicing and drying or when fresh | China and Japan |
| Oregon crab apple | used for making jelly | western North America Alaska and Aleutian Islands |
| Chinese pear-apple | fruits eaten fresh; of various shapes according to variety; Pellitzu is apple-shaped, but is called White Pear; cultivated | China |

* Illustrated on page 95.

50. Chickasaw plum or mountain cherry (*Prunus augustifolia*)

52. Sour cherry (*Prunus cerasus*)

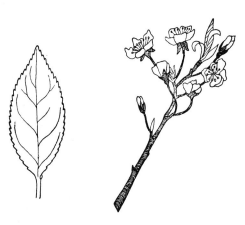

51. Cherry plum (*Prunus cerasifera*)

53. European bird cherry (*Prunus padus*)

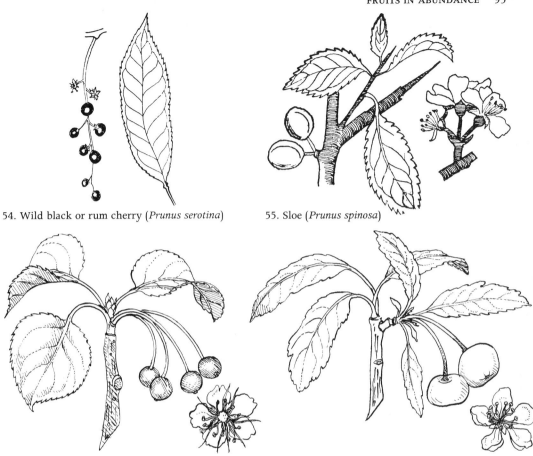

54. Wild black or rum cherry (*Prunus serotina*)    55. Sloe (*Prunus spinosa*)

56. *Left*: Chinese crab apple (*Pyrus baccata*); fragrant crap or crab apple (*Pyrus coronaria*)

similar to limao do matto. Fruits used for jams.
**Madruno.**    This tree grows in tropical parts
of the Americas. The yellow fruits have rough
surfaces and white pulp. They are slightly
aromatic and can be eaten raw, made into jams

and preserves. Sold in markets of Ecuador.
**Rhubarbs.**    There are several lesser-known
types of these fruits, produced from the leaf-
stalks and generally eaten cooked. See the
table below.

| RHUBARBS | | |
| --- | --- | --- |
| *Name* | *Product* | *Origin* |
| Tobolsk rhubarb | leaf stalks eaten after stewing | China and Siberia |
| sorrel rhubarb | | Mongolia |
| Himalaya rhubarb | | Himalayan region |

**Downy rose myrtle.**   A shrub of eastern India and Malaya. Fruits are used in pies.
**Sumachs.**   These belong to the species *Rhus*.

There are several which provide useful fruits. Shrubs and small trees. Some examples are given in the table below.

| SUMACHS | | |
|---|---|---|
| *Name* | *Product* | *Origin* |
| fragrant sumach, or sweet-scented sumach  shining or dwarf sumach | soaked berries are the source of a cooling drink | eastern North America |
| smooth or red sumach | fruits used in drinks; often mixed with maple sugar | eastern North America |
| squawberry or lemonade sumach | fruits used as food, fresh or dried, and made into jam, or into a beverage mixed with water | Mid-west of United States and northern Mexico |
| staghorn sumach or lemonade tree | fruits made into a drink known as 'Indian lemonade' | eastern North America |

**Currants.**   Plants of the species *Ribes*. There are a number of lesser-known but excellent shrub types, such as:

| CURRANT TYPES | | |
|---|---|---|
| *Name* | *Product* | *Origin* |
| American wild black currant | black berries used for jelly | eastern North America |
| golden currant, Missouri currant or buffalo currant | fruits used in jellies and pies having a characteristic taste; they were mixed with meat to make *pemmican* by American Indians | western North America |
| Alaskan currant | fruits eaten fresh or boiled or cooked with salmon roe | western North America |
| prickly or American gooseberry | berries used for pies, puddings and preserves | eastern North America |
| prickly currant | currants eaten fresh or dried | North America |
| smooth gooseberry | berries eaten in pies and used for making jam | eastern North America |
| swamp red currant | berries used for pies and jelly | eastern North America and Siberia |

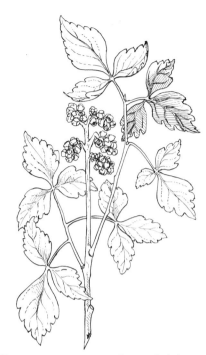

58. Shining or dwarf sumach (*Rhus copallina*)

57. Fragrant or sweet-scented sumach (*Rhus aromatica*)

59. Staghorn sumach or lemonade tree (*Rhus typhina*)

60. Golden, Missouri or buffalo currant (*Ribes aureum*)

**Rollinia.**   There are four species of these fruits found in South America, which produce edible fruits of good flavour, including caehiman and fructa da condessa. Trees and small tree, yielding edible fruits.

**Fructa de macaco.**   A Brazilian shrub or small tree, yeilding edible fruits.

**Californian rose.**   The ripe fruits of this rose shrub are eaten stewed or raw after frost has sweetened them. Much esteemed in Baja California. A western North America species.

**Rugosa rose.**   Eaten in Japan. Shrub.

**Apple rose.**   Similar to the rugosa rose, the hips are made into preserves and sauces and sometimes into a drink. Source of rosewine and rosehoney, both of which were known to the Romans. Much liked in Bavaria and Austria, where a tea substitute is made from the leaves called *'Deutscher Tee'*.

**Raspberry and Blackberry types.**   A large number of *Rubus* species berries are edible and eaten in different areas. Classed as shrubs. Some examples of useful plants are given in the table below.

61. Rugosa rose (*Rosa rugosa*)

| RASPBERRY AND BLACKBERRY TYPES | | |
|---|---|---|
| *Name* | *Product* | *Origin* |
| mora comun | well-flavoured fruits eaten fresh or cooked | Ecuador and Mexico |
| alleghany or mountain blackberry | berries made into jams, preserves or compotes | eastern North America |
| Chinese raspberry | large, red fruits of good flavour | China |
| Arctic bramble | Yellow fruits with pleasant taste | Arctic regions |
| Brazilian raspberry | Fruits eaten fresh and used in drinks; cultivated | Brazil |
| European dewberry | fruits used raw or in jellies and preserves | Europe |
| cloudberry, salmonberry or yellowberry | fruits much esteemed, eaten fresh or cooked; large quantities grow wild in woodlands | northern temperate hemisphere |
| Cochinchina raspberry | fruits eaten locally | China and Indo-China |

| | | |
|---|---|---|
| yellow Himalayan raspberry | fruit has a good raspberry flavour, used for preserves; it is sometimes called golden evergreen raspberry | eastern India, but naturalized in West Indies, Florida and California |
| mountain luzon | orange-yellow fruits of excellent taste | Philippines |
| Ecuador raspberry | good-quality fruits | Ecuador |
| northern dewberry | very variable species; fruits are often cultivated and are eaten raw, in jellies, jams and pies, used for juices, wines and syrups; one variety is called the Lucretia dewberry | eastern North America |
| Magellan raspberry | fruits are red and juicy and of large size; delicious taste | Falkland Islands |
| mora de Castilla | excellent quality fruits, from $\frac{3}{4}$–$1\frac{1}{2}$ inches long with good raspberry flavour; eaten fresh or used in preserves and for making a syrup called 'jaropa de mora'; very delicate flavour in some varieties | Ecuador and adjacent regions |
| Ichanga raspberry | small fruits of red colour and good taste | China |
| Canton raspberry | orange-red fruits eaten fresh | central and southern China |
| Colombian berry | very large fruits up to 2 inches long, tasting rather like loganberries | Colombia and Ecuador |
| Chinese yellow berry | large, yellow berries, eaten fresh | China and Japan |
| Molucca berry | good-flavoured fruits, eaten raw | found in Indo-China and Malaysia |
| mulberry-leaved raspberry | large, red berries | Japan |
| purple cane raspberry | sometimes cultivated; varieties include Gladstone, Shaffer and Philadelphia | eastern North America |
| black raspberry or black cap | cultivated | northern temperate areas |
| bramble or blackberry | fruits black; grows wild; used for jams, jellies or pies | northern temperate zone |
| Japanese raspberry | fruits eaten as raspberries | China and Japan |

| Philippine raspberry | bright red fruits, juicy and fine-flavoured, of good quality | Philippines and Japan |
| wine raspberry or wineberry | small fruits of cherry-red colour; cultivated | Japan |
| Mauritius raspberry or Cape bramble | fruits eaten fresh or cooked; cultivated | tropical Asia, but introduced in other regions |
| mora de rocoto or huagra mora | fruits resemble raspberries; used for drinks | Peru and Ecuador |
| southern dewberry | fruits used for jams and preserves or eaten fresh | North America |

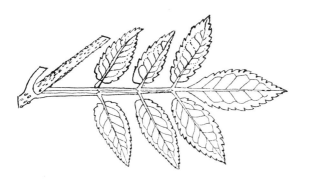

62. Elder (*Sambucus nigra*)

**Elders.** Belonging to *Sambucus* species, the southern elder, found in South America, the American elder of North America, the luiseno elder of western North America, the Australian and Mexican elders, the black or European elder, and the Peruvian elder all yield edible berries, used for making wine, jams, pies, preserves, jellies and syrups. Trees.

**Santol.** A species of the Philippines and Malaysia. Fruits eaten fresh, dried or candied. Tree.

**Doundaté.** Native to Africa, the fruits are deep red in colour and about 2 inches broad. The pulp is juicy and sweet. Shrub or small tree.

**Saurania.** A Mexican species, bearing edible fruits. Tree.

**Scaevola.** Fruits consumed in Australia. Perennial.

**Marvola nut.** A South African species, with fruits the size of plums, of good taste and excellent for making jellies. Tree.

**Silver buffalo berry.** The fruits are made into jelly, also eaten dried with sugar. May be stored for winter use and were cooked by American Indians with meat. Shrub. Native to North America.

**Russet buffalo berry.** Eaten dried or in cakes. Native to North America. Shrub.

**Solanums.** Nightshade family, which includes potatoes, aubergines and tomatoes. There are certain other interesting types. These are mainly shrubs and herbaceous plants. See the table opposite.

**White Beam, aria.**   A tree of Europe. The fruits are made into brandy and vinegar.

**Rowan, mountain ash.**   A European species, found also in west Siberia and Asia Minor, the fruits of this tree are eaten in jellies, preserved or in compotes. They are also made into a liqueur in Germany called *'Sechsamter-trophen'* and form an ingredient of some Russian vodkas.

**Service tree.**   Native to Europe, western Asia and North Africa. The fruits are eaten after the first touch of frost in autumn. They may also be made into wine. The apple-like Hayne type bears apple-shaped fruits, and the pear-like Hayne produces pear-shaped ones.

**Checker tree.**   Another European tree, which also grows in Asia Minor, Syria and North Africa. The fruits are used to make wine and brandy, as well as vinegar.

**Ambarella, otaheite apple.**   This is a tropical tree, which yields excellent fruits, suitable for jellies, preserves, marmalade, syrups and pickles. The fruits are known as Jew plums.

**Tonkin plum.**   A tropical Asian species which yields edible fruits. Tree.

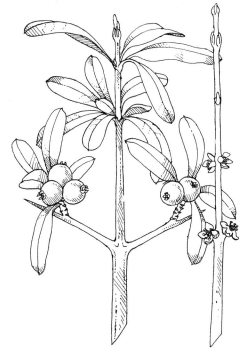

63. Silver buffalo berry (*Shepherdia argentea*)

| SOLANUMS | | |
| --- | --- | --- |
| *Name* | *Product* | *Origin* |
| Ethiopian apple ⎱ | ripe fruits eaten | Africa and Asia in warm regions |
| Brazilian apple ⎰ | | Brazil |
| kangeroo apple | fruits eaten raw, boiled or baked | Australia |
| African sunplant | yellow, bitter fruits, used in soup | tropical Africa |
| prickly sunplant | young fruits eaten raw with salt, often with codfish | central America and West Indies |
| elliptical sunplant | fruits eaten locally | South Australia |
| Malaysian sunplant ⎱ Indian sunplant ⎰ | fruits eaten in India and south-east Asia | south-east Asia |
| Guinea sunplant | fruits eaten locally | West Africa and the Guineas |

| | | |
|---|---|---|
| pepino | fruits frequently seedless, of greenish-yellow colour, round to oblong in shape, with purple-red blotches; good-tasting and juicy, rather aromatic and crisp, they are eaten raw; cultivated | Central and South America |
| Dahomey oliveplant | fruits eaten locally | West Africa and Congo region |
| olombe | fruits eaten locally | Gabon and neighbouring areas |
| Mexican apple | fruits are about as large as eggs, yellowish-green in colour and scented like apples; much esteemed in Mexico | Mexico |
| naranjillo | The fruits are round, about 2 inches in diameter, bright orange in colour, with thick, leathery skins and juicy, refreshing pulp; good for drinks and sherbets | Ecuador and Peru |
| zuni apple | fruits, when ripe are eaten raw, boiled or ground up, also mixed with red pepper and salt | British Columbia to Mexico |

**Yellow mombin, jobo, hog plum.** The fruits are of good quality and are usually eaten fresh. A tropical species. Tree.

**Mango plum.** Also a tropical type, cultivated in Indo-China. It produces edible fruits. Tree.

**Red mombin, Spanish plum.** A tropical American species. The fruits are called 'ciruela' or 'jocote' and are eaten fresh, boiled or dried. Sold in Mexico and Guatemala. Small tree.

**Hog plum, imbu.** A tree of north-east Brazil. The fruits have a fine flavour and may be eaten fresh or made into jelly. A popular Brazilian dessert called 'imbuzada' is made from the fruit boiled in sweetened milk. It also provides a beverage.

**Japanese staunton vine.** The white fruits are pulpy and sweet with a honey-like taste and are much appreciated in Japan, where the plant is cultivated. Woody vine.

**Myrobalans.** Called botanically *Terminalia* species, these plants furnish useful fruits. Two of the lesser-known kinds, which form trees are: *Bellerica terminalia* or Baleric myrobalan, a native of eastern India, Malaysia and the Philippines, which bears smooth, dark red, pleasant tasting fruits about $1\frac{1}{4}$ inches across, which are used for preserves; and New Guinea myrobalan, of which the almond-flavoured fruits are eaten locally.

**Harmand's grape.** A woody vine of south-east Asia, especially Malaya. The berries have a grape-like taste and are used for making jellies.

**Queensland apple.** The fruits of this species have the shape of a wild apple and are much esteemed locally. Native of southern and eastern Australia. Tree.

**Cardon de candelabro.** A dry-area species

of South America. In Argentina and Chile the fruits are made into brandy and syrup. Cactus type.

**Blueberries.** There are many of these shrub species producing valuable fruits. Some are given in the table below.

64. *Left*: mortino (*Vaccinium mortina*); low sweet or early sweet blueberry (*Vaccinium pennsylvanicum*)

| | BLUEBERRIES | |
|---|---|---|
| *Name* | *Product* | *Origin* |
| blueberry, swamp or high bush blueberry | fruits eaten fresh or canned and also used in pies and pastries; there is a range of improved cultivated varieties | eastern North America |
| dingleberry, mountain cranberry or bearberry | fruits used in jellies; flavour variable | south-eastern North America |
| Colombian blueberry, Andean blueberry or mortino | fruits much esteemed locally | Ecuador and Peru |
| Mexican blueberry | fruits used locally | Mexico |

| cranberry | fruits made into jelly; there are a number of cultivated varieties | eastern North America |
| bilberry | berries used locally for jellies, pies and tarts | Jamaica |
| mortino* | fruits eaten locally and sold in markets | Colombia and Ecuador |
| ground blueberry | fruits eaten in pies and compotes | North America |
| blueberry, European blueberry, whortleberry, bilberry | fruits are black, with a good bloom, of sweet to sweetish taste and may be eaten fresh, cooked and with milk, sugar or wine, used in pastries, compotes, syrup and sauce, and sometimes in soups; also the source of a wine called 'Heidelbierwein' or 'Heidelbiersekt', and a distilled beverage named 'Heidelbiergeist', and used to give wines a red colour | Europe and temperate Asia |
| bog bilberry | used to improve brandy | Europe and temperate Asia |
| myrtle bilberry | fruits used in preserves | Malaysia and Philippines |
| blueberry | fruits eaten locally | eastern North America |
| small cranberry | berries used as cranberries; grows wild | temperate and Arctic regions |
| low sweet blueberry or early sweet blueberry* | fruits consumed in pies, puddings or fresh; may also be dried for later use | eastern North America |
| cowberry or foxberry | berries are red in colour and can be made into sauces and jellies, sometimes substituted for cranberries | temperate zone |

* Illustrated on page 103.

**Wild spikenards, Solomon's plumes.** Berries eaten locally. A North American species. Perennial.

**Cranberry tree.** A small tree of Europe, North America and temperate parts of Asia. The fruits make good jellies and can be utilized instead of cranberries.

**Mooseberry viburnum.** A North American shrub. Fruits eaten fresh or preserved, especially in Alaska.

**Black haw, stag bush.** A North American plant, which bears edible fruits. They are best after having been touched by frost. Shrub.

**Chaste tree.** A Mediterranean species, noted for centuries as anti-aphrodisiac: the fruits are eaten for this purpose.

**African olive.** A tropical species bearing olive-like fruits, much esteemed locally. Tree.

**Mexican chaste tree.** Fruits eaten and sold in Mexico.

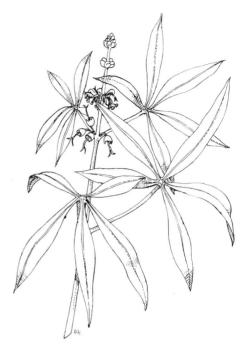

65. Black haw (*Viburnum prunifolium*)

66. Chaste tree (*Vitex agnus*)

**Summer grape.**  A woody vine, native to North America. The berries are edible. It is sometimes cultivated.

**Cape grape.**  Found in South Africa, this species bears purplish-black berries with reddish pulp. They are made into jelly locally. Woody vine.

**Caribbean grape.**  The fruits are sour but edible and can be used for jellies and jams. Found in the West Indies and North America. Woody vine.

**Spiny vitis.**  This plant produces black globose berries with a harsh taste. Sometimes cultivated in China. Woody vine.

**Fox grape.**  An eastern North American species. The plants are cultivated and the berries eaten raw or made into grape juice, syrup, jelly, jam, used for flavouring ice cream and candies or sweets, or for making into wine and beverages of non-alcoholic content. There are various varieties, such as Catawba, Concord, Isabella, Niagara, Delaware and Worden. Woody vine.

**African grape.**  Various species, natives of tropical Africa, produce edible berries, which are eaten fresh or preserved. Woody vines.

**Abinsi grape.**  A West African plant which bears edible berries, sold in local markets. They are eaten raw or in soups. Woody vine.

**Muscadine grape or southern fox grape.**  A species of the eastern United States, generally cultivated. There are several varieties. Fruits are eaten fresh. Woody vine.

**Frost grape, river bank grape.**  This plant bears edible fruits and is sometimes cultivated. It is a North American species. Woody vine.

**Willughbeia.**  Native to Indo-China, Malaysia and the Himalayan region, this bears ovoid fruits the size of lemons and of yellowish colour. They are eaten locally. Woody vine.

**Tallow wood.** The fruits are about the size of plums and are widely eaten, being sometimes pickled. A tree of the tropics and subtropics.

**Zalacca, salak.** An East Indian species which bears reddish-brown and sweet fruits. They can be eaten when ripe, but the young fruits are pickled. These fruits are also preserved in cans with salt water and eaten by Muslim pilgrims going to Mecca. Low, almost stemless palm plant.

**Jujubes.** These are *Zizyphus* species, all small trees, which bear edible fruits. Some useful types are given in the table below.

## Culture of Fruits

For purposes of cultivation or growing, fruits may be roughly divided into three main classes: trees, shrubs, and vines or small plants. Fruit trees are treated in gardening or farming as orchard types. They need proper

|  | JUJUBES | |
| --- | --- | --- |
| *Name* | *Product* | *Origin* |
| Mexican jujube | edible fruits, eaten locally | Mexico |
| Joazeiro jujube | | Brazil |
| common jujube or Chinese jujube | fruits are ovoid, with thin, dark skins and whitish, mealy flesh of sweet, pleasant flavour; they may be eaten fresh or dried like dates, cooked with rice or millet or in honey or syrup, stewed, boiled or baked, made into glacé fruit or jujube bread; there are several good varieties, such as Yu, Lang, Mushinghong | eastern India and Malaysia; also introduced into other Asian lands and the Mediterranean region |
| lotus jujube | edible fruits, known to the ancient inhabitants of Lybia as lotus, hence the name lotophages, or lotus-lovers (eaters), applied to these peoples in classical times | North Africa |
| Mauritanian jujube | edible fruits called *'tsa'* or Chinese dates | tropical Asia and Africa |
| mistol or Argentine jujube | sweet and juicy berries are used in Bolivia for the preparation of the local beverage called *'chicha'* | Andean region |
| buffalo or Cape thorn | edible fruits eaten locally | southern and tropical Africa |
| Christ's thorn or crown of thorns | fruits, eaten when dried, have the flavour of shrivelled apples | North Africa and Arabia |

67. Christ's thorn or crown of thorns (*Zizyphus spina-christi*)

spacing, according to size, and regular mulching and pruning. In addition, spraying against insect pests with safe, non-toxic materials, such as pyrethrum, may be necessary. In hot and dry areas, irrigation is frequently essential. Climbing fruit plants, such as melon types, require supports and should generally speaking be treated in a similar way to cucumber substitutes. High humidity can cause rotting and falling of vine fruits, with a heavy incidence of moulds and mildew, called in garden terms 'damping-off'. On the other hand, excessive dryness, both of the air and the soil, is undesirable. Water requirements are high, because the transpiration rate from the leaves is appreciable, so to avoid wilting, care must be taken to ensure that the plants get ample moisture in the root zone at all times. Hand-pollination is often essential for crops

grown under glass; out-of-door fruits are normally pollinated by insects. Shelter from strong wind and shading during very hot periods from sun-scorch are benefical to the good culture of vine fruits.

When growing small fruit plants, it is a good plan to start them from runners, if these are produced by the species concerned. As a rule, many such types require a good supply of potash and phosphates, while waterlogging should be avoided. Excessive moisture around the root crowns will cause the lower leaves and stems to rot. It must always be remembered that the object in fruit growing is to produce large, succulent and unblemished specimens, so manuring should concentrate on the output of produce and not on heavy foliage development. This means, in practice, a moderate level of nitrogen, especially just before the period when bearing starts, as well as in the last stages of fruiting. Mulching is most beneficial, since the composts or farmyard manures used are fairly low in nitrogen and the potash and phosphates can be increased quickly by dressings of ammonium sulphate or superphosphate at the rate of 1–2 ounces per square yard, well mixed in with the mulch. Most fruit types, especially the smaller plants, are surface feeders and will soon respond to this treatment.

## Cooking

Most fruits are highly enjoyable when served raw. This also minimizes loss of vitamins and minerals. Where it is necessary to prepare raw fruits ahead of time, browning caused by oxygen coming into contact with the exposed flesh can be checked by dipping them in a weak sugar solution, and if possible leaving them in a refrigerator or cool place, until required for the table.

Stewing or simmering should always be done in just a little water and at low heat. Rapid boiling spoils fruits and adversely affects the shape of the cooked material. Dried fruits should be soaked in water for some hours before cooking to rehydrate them and make them tender. Another good way to prepare some fruits is to bake them in the oven. Fruits can also be boiled or fried or stewed in wines. Pies of different fruits are popular too, while excellent ice creams and sherbets, as well as squashes and drinks, can be included, in menus. Mention must also be made of salads, jams, preserves, bottled and canned fruits, jellies, and puddings produced from various sorts of fruits. Recipes will be found in good cookery books.

**Dried fruits.** Fruits can be sun-dried or artificially dehydrated. The quality may be judged by their colour and appearance. The best have a bright hue for their type, are firm but flexible, and a fresh, pleasant smell. Dried fruits should be stored in closed containers, free from damp, and must not be allowed to become musty or infested by insects.

**Storage.** Fruits which keep for reasonable periods, when fresh, can be stored on shelves in clean rooms, free from excessive dust, damp, and bright light. Good ventilation is essential, without too high temperatures, or any frost during winter-time. Do not put banana-type produce in the refrigerator because the near-freezing conditions will make it go dark brown and soft suddenly. Prepared fruits may, however, be quick-frozen in the normal manner, although when defrosted they tend to be rather watery and must be eaten without delay. Bruised or damaged fruits should never be kept in store.

**Fruit products.** Amongst the many products derived from fruits, which can be prepared in the home, using lesser-known types, are pickles, sauces, purées, and beverages, as well as candied fruits and fondues.

# Chapter 8

# EDIBLE FLOWERS

The flowers of various plants can be eaten and are much relished in different countries, either as items of food or for flavouring purposes. Not only can we make special salads and preserves from different blooms, but we can also utilize them in preparing attractive and nutritious dishes and drinks in our homes. This aspect of cookery is today much neglected and it would be a real contribution to domestic science, gardening and household management if it was revived. Here is a list of flowers that are used for food throughout the world:

**Sweet violet.**  A perennial herb, native to Europe and Asia. It is often cultivated. Tea made from violet leaves is excellent for coughs. The flowers may be candied and used in confections and sweets.

68. Sweet violet (*Viola odorata*)

**Early blue or palmate violet, wild okra.**  This species grows in eastern North America. The plant is very mucilaginous and is used for thickening soups. Perennial.

**Primrose.**  Various species provide flowers and leaves used to make primrose or cowslip tea, used for a home remedy. Perennials.

**Common nasturtium.**  A herbaceous vine, the flowering buds of which are used for flavouring vinegar, and also in place of capers. Widely grown, and sometimes called Indian cress.

**Marigolds.**  The flowers are employed in making calendula tea, which is stimulating and a useful home remedy. Annual.

**Roses.**  The eglantine rose bears flowers that are the source of a sweet called gulangabin, composed of rose petals and honey. This is a shrub native to Asia Minor, the northern Middle East and the Punjab in India.

**Abutilon.**  The flowers are eaten as a vegetable in Brazil. The plant is a shrub, suited to warm regions.

**Bananas.**  The young flower heads of various banana species are consumed as vegetables in different countries. In China they are made into pickles.

**Indian butter tree, illipe, mahwa.**  A species found in India, especially Bengal, and south-east Asia. The creamy white petals of the flowers are eaten fresh or dried for later consumption. In India, the fleshy petals are harvested in the early months of the year, the yield per tree being about 200 lb. It has been estimated that the annual production of Indian butter tree flowers is about 25,000 tons. An alcoholic beverage named mahua spirit is also distilled from the flowers. There is another species, termed mee tree, which also yields flowers of similar value.

**Red cotton tree.** This is a tree of Malaya and Burma. The fleshy calyces of the large red-coloured flowers are consumed as a curry vegetable. Much esteemed locally.

**Phogalli.** Flowers are eaten in northern India after drying and grinding into flour, which is then made into bread. Also cooked with butter or ghee.

**Rozelle, Jamaica sorell.** A *Hibiscus* species. The red, fleshy calyces are made into jellies and sauces. Varieties include Victor, Archer and Rico. Cultivated in tropical areas.

**Moonflower.** A beautiful tropical bloom, which is eaten as a vegetable. Climber.

**Thunberg's lily.** Often used in China for its flowers. Regarded as a table delicacy. Bulb.

**Rivea.** A woody vine, the fleshy flowers of which are eaten. Tropical.

**Agati.** This is the agati sesbania tree, native to south-east Asia and northern Australia. The flowers are used in salads and as pot herbs, as well as being much relished when boiled or fried.

**Japanese and Indian chrysanthemums.** The flowerheads are either dried and preserved for later use, eaten boiled or pickled in vinegar.

**Spicy cedar.** An African species, the fragrant flowers of which are employed to flavour rice and other foods. Tree.

**Yuccas.** The flowers of the Mohave yucca of California and neighbouring areas are used as food. They are boiled and made into vegetable dishes. The whitle yucca is eaten in similar manner, likewise the ozote and datil yuccas, natives of Mexico.

**Mioga ginger.** A Japanese ginger plant which has a bergamot-like flavour. The young flowers are consumed locally. Perennial.

**Aoso, shiroso.** This plant belongs to the species *Perilla*, an annual herb of Japanese origin. The flower clusters are eaten after salting.

**Sargent lily.** Flowers eaten in China. Perennial.

**Jumpy bean (Leucaena glauca).** A woody plant of the tropics. The flowerheads are used as a side-dish in Java with rice.

**Chufle.** A Mexican and South American species. The young flower clusters are cooked and eaten as a vegetable. Sold in local markets. Very similar is violet chufle, a related plant. Perennials.

**Karatas.** The very young inflorescences are eaten in El Salvador as a vegetable. Perennial.

**Langwas or greater galangal.** This is a plant of tropical Asia. It is often cultivated. The flowers are eaten raw, sometimes with other vegetables or in pickles, especially in Java. Perennial.

**Cymbidium.** Belonging to the family of orchids, this Japanese species produces flowers that are consumed after they have been salted or preserved in plum vinegar. They are also made into a drink with hot water. Perennial.

**Annam plum.** The flower clusters are eaten as a vegetable or in salads. This species grows in the tropics and is a native of eastern Asia.

**Opuntia.** The flowers of the cactus *Opuntia basiliana*, a shrub of south-western North America, are eaten after steaming.

**Geonoma.** The young flower clusters are cooked and eaten in Mexico. Palm.

**Chamlagu.** This is the Chinese pea tree or shrub, which is indigenous to north China and therefore can withstand cold conditions. The yellow flowers are eaten locally.

**Heracleum.** This plant is found in North America. The young flowers are consumed locally. One popular name is Indian cow parsnip. The roots resemble rutabaga in taste. Perennial.

**Red bud.** A small tree of North America.

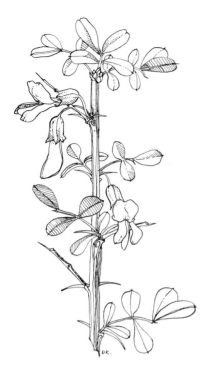

69. Chamlagu (*Caragana chamlagu*)

The flowers were first used by French Canadians in salads and pickles.

**Spondias.** The flower clusters are eaten as a vegetable or in salads. Found in tropical Asia and cultivated in Indo-China.

## Culture of Flowers

To produce really good flowers for consumption, it is necessary to try and give some protection, where this is practicable, against damage by weather. Strong winds, heavy rain, excessive cold and related inclement conditions can destroy flowers easily. The general points to observe when growing edible flowers are very much the same as those listed for vegetables or for fruits. Much, of course, depends on the particular types in question. Because of their delicate construction, flowers can be damaged quickly and therefore care should be taken when harvesting produce.

## Cooking

Edible flowers are prepared in various ways, according to the dishes in which they are to be consumed, or the manner of their usage. Often, they are eaten as vegetables, mixed into salads, preserved or incorporated in pickles, or form the basis of sweets and confections. Appropriate cookery books should be consulted, especially those which deal with exotic dishes. Alternatively, it is always a safe rule to follow the general guidelines of preparation for the class of food required, that is to say, when using flowers as a vegetable, cook as for vegetables, or when as a confection, use in a similar way to other confectionary materials.

# Chapter 9

# VIGOUR FROM NUTS

The term 'nut' is usually applied to that class or type of fruit that consists generally of a kernel enclosed in a hard shell. A great number of nuts are commercially important today, principally as articles of food or for the oils that they yield. It is popularly supposed that eating nuts imparts vigour to people and, as with many other folk stories and traditions, there may well be a good deal of truth in this idea, because apart from their carbohydrate and fat content, nuts do provide a useful addition of protein to the human diet (particularly for vegetarians), as well as minerals and some vitamins.

Nevertheless, by and large, nut eating has declined within recent decades. There has, of course, been a great increase in the extraction of oils for making margarines and soaps, but the consumption of fresh, raw nuts and nut flour has dropped. In earlier times, man made far more use of nuts both in his own food pattern and for the nourishment of his farm and domestic livestock. In the Middle Ages, when Europe was a peasant society, vast herds of pigs and other animals were fed on the acorns, chestnuts, walnuts and beech seeds or mast produced by the huge forests that then covered most of the continent. This method of supplying farm stock with nutriment has to some extent continued even nowadays in certain areas. For example, in Portugal use is still made of the cork oak forests to provide fodder for fattening swine, while in the southern states of the USA, hogs are brought to

70. Beechnut (*Fagus sylvatica*)

a marketable condition largely on a diet of nuts. In England, where at one time the produce of beech trees was regarded as important in the agricultural calendar, the use of this foodstuff has generally been forgotten and it just goes to waste. However, in some parts of Europe, a salad oil is extracted from beech mast.

Roman soldiers on garrison duty along Hadrian's wall in ancient Britain used the flour of pinenuts as a regular portion of their daily rations. It was made into nutritious cakes. Pine seeds are still important in Italy, where they are sold for export as pignolia. Another valuable nut is the filbert or hazel, of which there are many species, while in China the water chestnut and the singharanut are important sources of human food, being rich in starch.

Generally speaking, today we neglect our nuts as sources of nutritious food. Only vegetarians make proper use of them. This is a great pity, because nuts can be good substitutes for meat and to some extent for cereals. Moreover, nut trees require much less attention than do common farm and garden crops. Often it is possible to collect great quantities of nuts at no cost from wild trees and plants spread throughout the countryside or growing in forests and hedgerows. Because few people bother to harvest these crops they simply go to waste, year after year, and represent a serious loss of good and wholesome food.

## Lesser-known Types of Nuts

Better-known nuts, such as chestnuts, walnuts, brazilnuts, hazelnuts and almonds are familiar to most people, although they only eat them very occasionally. But there are numerous kinds of less well-known types that never come to general notice. These include both different species of the popular nuts already mentioned and a whole range of what we might term obscure nuts. These latter are nevertheless very important in their own localities and have distinctive economic attributes which are worthy of special attention. It has been said that if you have a good nut tree in your garden or beside your house, you have an asset for life that will stand you in good stead at all times and provide a useful food supply in emergencies or during periods of scarcity. Here are some useful lesser-known nut-bearing plants that can provide nutritious food in different areas:

71. Araucarian pinenut or arauco (*Araucaria imbricata*)

**Parana pine.** Also called Brazilian pine, this species is found in Paraguay, Argentina and Brazil. The seeds are edible and are sold in local markets. Tree.

**Araucarian pinenut, arauco.** A species found on the coastal cordillera of Chile. The seeds, called pinones or pinons, are eaten roasted. Tree.

**Ramon breadnut.** A species of tropical America. The seeds are eaten after roasting. Tree.

**Walnuts.** There are a number of lesser-known species, which have in some cases greater value than the common or European walnut, which often fails to withstand harsher growing conditions. A selection is given in the table overleaf.

**Chestnuts.** Japanese and Chinese chestnuts are hardier than the European species. Nuts are much eaten locally.

**Castanopsis nut.** A warm-area species which produces nuts resembling chestnuts in outward appearance and oaks in seed. Often eaten and taste rather like a cross between chestnut and acorn. The nuts can be consumed boiled, parched or roasted. Different types include Tonkin chestnut, golden-leaved chestnut or golden chinquapin, Sumatra castanopsis, Philippine chestnut or chinquapin, Chinese and Tibetan chinquapins and Henry chinquapin, amongst others. Sometimes, in older books, the *Castanopsis* species are

| | LESSER-KNOWN WALNUTS | |
|---|---|---|
| *Name* | *Product* | *Origin* |
| Bolivian black walnut | nuts of good quality | Bolivia |
| Cathay walnut | nuts eaten in China | central China |
| butternut, long or white walnut | nuts used as food; sugar may be extracted from the sap of this species | eastern North America |
| Chinese walnut | fruits eaten locally and cultivated in China | mountainous regions of Asia, western China |
| nogal or Ecuador walnut | thick-shelled nuts, of which the rich, tasty kernels are made into sweetmeats called *'nogada de ibarra'*. | Ecuador Highlands |
| Kamaonia walnut | nuts eaten locally as food | central and west Himalayan regions |
| Manchurian walnut | nuts eaten locally | Manchuria |
| Guatemalan walnut | nuts consumed locally | Guatemala and Mexico |
| black walnut | nuts used as food | eastern United States and Canada |
| Texas walnut | nuts eaten locally | south-west of United States and northern Mexico |
| Siebold walnut | nuts consumed locally | Japan and China |
| heartnut | nuts used as food | Japan |

| | LESSER-KNOWN FILBERTS OR HAZELS | |
|---|---|---|
| *Name* | *Product* | *Origin* |
| Constantinople or Turkish hazelnut | nuts used locally | south-eastern Europe to south-western Siberia |
| Siberian hazelnut | nuts eaten locally | China, Siberia and Japan |
| beaked hazelnut | nuts used as food | eastern North America |
| Lambert's filbert | large nuts, sometimes cultivated; varieties are Ceret, Large Long Spanish | southern Europe |
| American hazelnut | | eastern North America |
| California hazelnut | nuts consumed locally | west coast of the United States |
| giant hazelnut | | Europe |

72. Chile hazel (*Guevina avellana*)

73. Giant hazelnut (*Corylus maxima*)

classed as *Castanea* species, but modern terminology prefers the former description. Trees.

**Chile hazel.** A Chilean plant, which bears pleasant-flavoured seeds, resembling hazelnuts. Much esteemed locally. Tree.

**Chufa, rush nut, earthnut, earth almond, ground almond, yellow nut grass.** This species is cosmopolitan, but is notable in southern Europe. Used for food. Perennial.

**Cobnut of Jamaica.** A plant of the West Indies and tropical America. Eaten locally.

**Dika nut.** Grows in West Africa. Eaten locally. Also Gabon dika, a related type.

**Filberts or hazels.** Small trees or shrubs. The nuts are roundish or oblong, of yellow-brown colour, and have a medium-thin shell and a single kernel. There are various species growing in different regions of much interest and food value. See the table opposite for a selection.

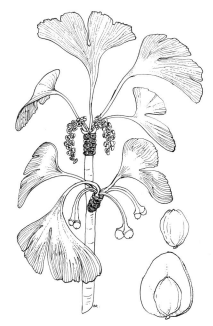

74. Gingkonut or maidenhair tree (*Gingko biloba*)

**Ginkgo nut.** A species of China and Japan. Often grown around Buddhist temples and thought to be a great delicacy. In Europe it is called the maidenhair tree. The seeds are eaten roasted.

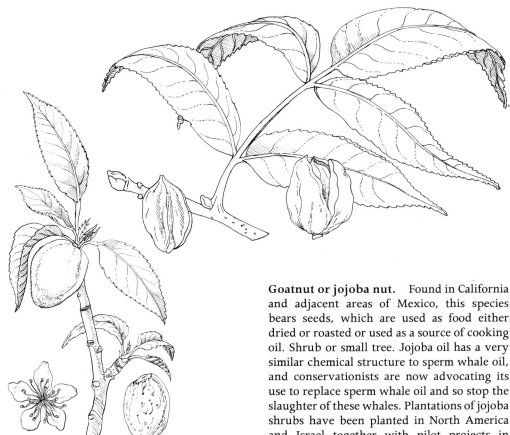

75. *Left*: almond (*Amygdalus communis*); pecan (*Carya* spp.)

**Hickories or pecans.** These are American trees, of several kinds. The Illinois nut or commercial pecan is the choicest and best known, the seeds being sold extensively. Other types are given in the table opposite.

**Java almond.** A tree of the East Indies and Pacific region. The nuts have a pleasant taste and are eaten often with rice or in pastries. Much esteemed locally.

**Pilinut.** A tree of the Philippines. The seeds, after roasting, have a good taste and are used in confectionary. Related to Java almond.

**Goatnut or jojoba nut.** Found in California and adjacent areas of Mexico, this species bears seeds, which are used as food either dried or roasted or used as a source of cooking oil. Shrub or small tree. Jojoba oil has a very similar chemical structure to sperm whale oil, and conservationists are now advocating its use to replace sperm whale oil and so stop the slaughter of these whales. Plantations of jojoba shrubs have been planted in North America and Israel together with pilot projects in Mexico and Australia.

**Moreton Bay chestnut, Moreth Bay chestnut.** This plant produces edible seeds. It is found in Queensland and New South Wales. Tree.

**Nittanut.** These nuts are produced by *Parkia* species in Africa. The seeds are edible and are used locally, having a high protein content.

**Oyster nut tree, tabui, krobonko.** Seeds are eaten cooked. An African species.

**Pinenuts.** These trees often grow in remote and arid regions. The seeds are born in the axils of the cone scales. They are fairly rich in oil and have a pleasant taste. Some useful types are given in the table opposite.

HICKORIES OR PECANS

| Name | Product | Origin |
| --- | --- | --- |
| Chinese hickory | nuts eaten locally | east China |
| pignut hickory | nuts, variable in quality | eastern North America |
| big shellbark hickory | nuts used as food | central and eastern United States |
| shagbark hickory or shellbark hickory | nuts used as food | eastern United States and south-east Canada |
| mockernut or big-bud hickory | nuts consumed locally | eastern United States and Ontario |
| nutmeg hickory | | south-western United States |
| black hickorynut | | Texas, Arkansas and Oklahoma |
| Carolina hickorynut | nuts eaten locally | south-eastern United States |
| Fernow hickorynut | | south-western United States |
| hammock hickorynut | | south-eastern United States |
| red hickorynut | | eastern United States and Onatario |

PINENUTS

| Name | Product | Origin |
| --- | --- | --- |
| white bark pinenut | large, sweet seeds | Pacific coast of North America |
| Swiss stone pinenut* | seeds eaten in Europe; used in pastries and milk foods | central Europe, north-west Russia, north Asia and Amur region in Siberia |
| nut pine, Mexican pinon | large, oily seeds are important local food | south-west of United States, and northern Mexico |
| Coulter pinenut* | seeds eaten locally | California |
| nut pine or pinon | seeds consumed locally | south-western United States and north of Mexico |
| Chilghoza pinenut | seeds eaten locally | Afghanistan, Himalayan region of India |
| Korean pinenut | seeds used locally | Korea and Kamtchatka |
| sugar pinenut* | | Pacific coast of United States |

* Illustrated overleaf.

| | | |
|---|---|---|
| nut pine pinon | seeds are important food locally | south-west United States and Baja California |
| western white pinenut | seeds eaten locally | north-western United States and British Columbia |
| Parry pinenut | important food locally | California |
| western yellow pinenut | nuts eaten locally | western North America and northern Mexico |
| digger or bull pinenut | source of local food | California |
| Torrey's pinenut | large seeds are eaten roasted | California |

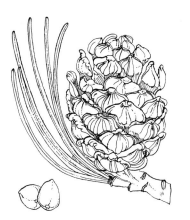

76. Swiss stone pinenut (*Pinus cembra*)

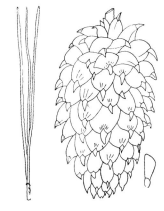

77. Coulter pinenut (*Pinus coulteri*)

78. Sugar pinenut
(*Pinus lambertiana*)

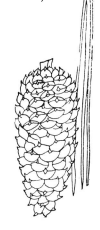

79. Western yellow pinenut
(*Pinus lambertiana*)

80. Limber pinenut (*Pinus flexilis*)

Other species yielding edible nuts include Jeffrey pine, lacebark pine, limber pine, Ponderosa pine, whitebark pine and singleleaf pine.

**Quandong nut.** An Australian species, seeds of pleasant taste. Tree.

**Queensland nut.** Also called Australian hazel, this plant bears seeds which have an excellent taste when roasted. Found mostly in Queensland and New South Wales. Tree.

**Paradise or Sapucaia nut.** A South American species, with good quality nuts. Tree.

**Suari nut.** A tree of Brazil and Guyana, which produces oily nuts. Sometimes cultivated. Has been introduced into other regions.

**Tropical almond, tavola nut, myrobalan, almendro, Indian almond or Demerara almond.** This species provides excellent nuts of delicious flavour. The tree gives two crops annually. A Malaysian tree, introduced into other areas.

**Okari.** A tree of Papua and New Britain, which furnishes large nuts about 3 inches long by $\frac{3}{4}$ inch in diameter. Flavour and quality are excellent.

## Culture of Nuts

There are many types of nut-producing species, with differing characteristics and adaptability to varying conditions. In general, nut-yielding trees and shrubs may be considered, in garden practice, as plants requiring ample phosphates, to aid the formation of seeds. Mulching is always beneficial, with regular pruning and protection from insect pests. Considered as a horticultural crop, nuts are orchard specimens, receiving much the same attention as fruits. Nut groves or plantations should not be left uncared for, but should be kept clear of weeds and heavy undergrowth, which inhibit the good growth of the plants.

## Cooking

Nuts can be eaten fresh, straight out of the shell, or incorporated into various dishes.

When buying or collecting nuts it is essential to examine the produce very carefully. Because of their hard exteriors it is often difficult to judge the condition of nuts by eye alone. Apparently good lots may have dry or withered kernels, so it is advisable to shake a few specimens vigorously. If they rattle, you may be sure that the seeds are old and of poor quality. Again, the presence of mites or small insects like weevils are signs that the produce is in bad condition and should be rejected. In the trade, the standards of inspection that may apply to fruits and vegetables are often neglected in the case of nuts, so many low-class lots are offered for sale and bought by unsuspecting customers.

Amongst interesting dishes that may be made from different sorts of nuts are:

**Nut mince.** Made from a mixture of minced or finely chopped nuts, butter, breadcrumbs, onion, sauce and stock, and served with mashed potatoes and croûtons.

**Walnut roast.** Prepared from milled walnuts, breadcrumbs, onion, margarine, gravy, and condiments.

**Walnut trifle.** Made from walnuts, bananas or substitute, breadcrumbs, raspberry jam, custard, angelica and cherries.

**Nut bread.** An ordinary bread mixture containing chopped nuts.

**Nut buns.** Prepared from a plain bun or scone mixture with added chopped nuts.

**Nut cakes.** Similar to nut buns, but using standard cake mixtures of different types.

**Nutty meringues.** Ordinary meringue mixture with added chopped and blanched nuts.

Nut flours can be made by milling or grinding up nuts and constitute a nutritious and palatable food. Nuts can be added to salads, used in biscuits, or as an ingredient of sandwich fillings. It has been said that if every child in the less-developed Third World were to be supplied with two or three ounces of nuts daily, the main problem of protein deficiency would disappear.

# Chapter 10

# BEVERAGES IN PLENTY

The range of good beverages that can be prepared from plants is very wide. Broadly speaking, these liquids may be divided into non-alcoholic and alcoholic beverages. The second type is often obtained from the first by suitable processing.

## Non-alcoholic Drinks

Here is a list of little-known plant species which provide pleasant-tasting and often nutritious drinks:

**Actophila.**  A species of tropical Asia. A palatable beverage is obtained from the flowers and leaves. Shrub.

**Actinella.**  This plant is found in the southwestern areas of the United States. The flower tops are used to produce a beverage consumed locally. Perennial.

**Baobab.**  Also called monkey bread, Ethiopian sour bread, cream of tartar tree and various other names, this species is native to tropical Africa, but is found in other areas. The pulp of the fruits is made into a beverage. There are related species in Australia and Madagascar. Trees.

**Giant hyssup.**  This species grows in Missouri and western areas of the United States. A decoction of the leaves is made into a beverage. Perennial.

**Java or Philippine galangal.**  The sap of this plant is cooked with sugar or honey and water added to form a refreshing drink. Perennial.

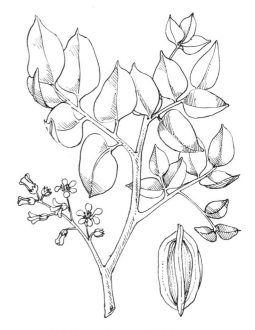

81. Carambola (*Averrhoa carambola*)

**Desert lemon.**  An Australian tree, native to Queensland and New South Wales. The fruits are the source of a lemonade substitute.

**Aubrya.**  A drink called *'stouton'* is prepared from the fruits of this African species. Woody plant.

**Carambola.**  The fruits are used to make a refreshing squash drink. Native of tropical Asia, but introduced into other regions. Small tree.

**Peach palm.** A plant of South America, often cultivated in Brazil. The peach-like fruits are made into a pleasant drink. Tree.

**Yage.** A climber or liane, indigenous to South America, and found especially in Brazil. The leaves and twigs are the source of a beverage called *'ayahuasca'*. Excessive quantities are said to cause a telepathic effect on the drinkers.

**Bidens.** Found in the south-west United States and adjacent areas of Mexico, this plant bears flower tops from which a thirst-quenching beverage is made. Perennial.

**Ramon breadnut tree.** A native of Guiana. The seeds can be used as a substitute for coffee, after roasting and grinding.

**Cow tree.** Another tropical American species. The latex is produced by making slits in the trunk of this tree and can be drunk mixed with water as a milk substitute.

**Arabian or Abyssinian tea.** A small shrub, native to Ethiopia, but also cultivated in southern Arabia. The leaves and twigs are used locally, after drying, to form a tea substitute. When they are mixed with honey a palatable wine is produced. At one time, this drink was prohibited by the Prophet Mohammed, but a later decree permitted its consumption on the grounds that its use only produced hilarity and good humour.

**Palo verde.** This species is found in the south-west United States and Baja California. The seeds are used for making a local beverage. Small tree.

**Quinoa.** This plant grows in South America, especially in Chile and Peru, where it has for long been cultivated. The seeds are made into a drink called *'tschitscha'*. Annual.

**Citrus species.** Popular citrus fruits include oranges, lemons and grapefruits. Many of the lesser-known types, such as hystrix lemon, sweet lime, Ninmeng or Canton lemon, tamisan, citron, musk lime, calamondin, king orange and kalpi, are the source of excellent squashes and substitute orange/lemonades.

**Coffees.** A number of lesser-known species produce coffee drinks or substitutes. A selection is given in the table below.

LESSER-KNOWN COFFEES

| Name | Product | Origin |
|------|---------|--------|
| Arnold's coffee | | Congo area |
| Breviceps coffee | | tropical Africa |
| Canephora coffee | | Congo area |
| Congensis coffee (variety Chaloti Pierre) | beans made into coffee | Congo area |
| Dewevrei's coffee | | tropical Africa |
| Excelsa coffee | | Gulf of Guinea and Congo |
| Humboldt's coffee | | Gulf of Guinea and Congo |
| Liberian coffee | | west and central Africa, India, Ceylon, West Indies and Guyana |
| Maclaud's coffee | seeds which do not contain caffeine | Guinea |
| Quillon coffee | | Congo area |
| highland coffee | small berries | Sierra Leone, West Indies, India and Ceylon |

The products of certain other plants can also be used as coffee substitutes, after drying and roasting: see the table below.

COFFEE SUBSTITUTES

| Name | Product used for making coffee drink |
| --- | --- |
| quackgrass | rootstock |
| asparagus, garden type | seeds |
| Spanish vetch | seeds |
| Senegal boscia | seeds |
| ramon breadnut tree | seeds |
| smooth senna | seeds |
| silly senna | seeds |
| coffee senna or mogdad (negro coffee) | seeds |
| tora or sickle senna | seeds |
| chestnuts | seeds or nuts |
| carob | seeds |
| chick pea or garbanzos | seeds |
| chicory | roots |
| hawthorns, including European may tree | seeds |
| carrots | roots |
| lutea yam | tubers |
| catchweed or goose-grass | fruits |
| soyabean | seeds |
| Kentucky coffee tree | seeds |
| two-rowed barley | seeds or grains |
| setosa iris | seeds |
| Alaskan lathryus | seeds |
| Leontodon | roots |
| ibota privet | seeds |
| Japanese privet | seeds |
| African locust bean (café du Sudan) | seeds |
| juniper mistletoe | seeds |
| Texas tamarind | seedcoats |
| scorzonera | roots |
| rye | seeds or grains |
| holy thistle | seeds |
| pignut or goatnut | seeds |
| chervin or skirret | roots |
| rowan tree or European mountain ash | dried fruits |
| dandelion | roots |

82. Kentucky coffee tree (*Gymnocladus canadensis*)

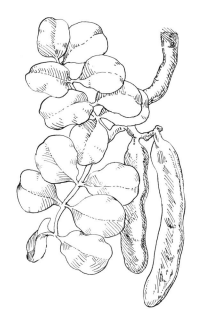

83. Carob (*Ceratonia siliqua*)

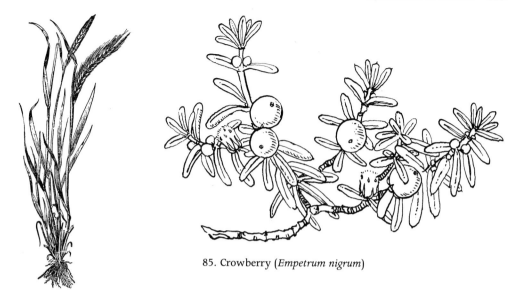

85. Crowberry (*Empetrum nigrum*)

84. Rye (*Secale cereale*)

**Cola.**   There are several species, natives of Africa, which produce nuts used for making beverages, sold commercially under various trade names.

**Coreopsis.**   Whole plant used to make decoction for producing a pleasant drink. The species is found in the southern and the midwestern United States. Annual.

**Tuhu.**   A small tree, indigenous to New Zealand. The berries are made into a drink locally, but the shoots should not be eaten.

**Chufa, earth almond, yellow nut grass.**   A cosmopolitan plant. The tubers, when pressed, yield a juice that is made into a drink called *'horchata de chufas'*.

**Texas sotol.**   The central part of the bud of this plant contains a sugary pulp that can be made into a drink called 'sotol'. Wheeler sotol is a similar plant. Both are natives of Texas, New Mexico and Arizona. Perennials.

**Crowberry.**   A small shrub, found in temperate Europe, Asia and North America. The edible berries may be made into a beverage when mixed with sour milk. This is popular in Iceland.

**Genipa, marmalade box.**   A tropical American species. The fruits are the source of a drink called *'genipado'*, which is said to have very refreshing properties. Tree.

**Igara gladiolus.**   An African species, the corms of which are made into a cooling beverage. Perennial.

**Thunberg's hydrangea.**   The young leaves are harvested, then steamed and rolled, followed by drying. The product is made into a sweet drink, called *'amacha'* ('sweet tea') in Japan. Shrub.

**Oregon grape.**   A western North American shrub which yields fruits that are used for making a substitute lemonade. (*Illustrated overleaf.*)

**Marumia.**   A woody vine, found in western areas of Java. The berries are made into a pleasant drink.

86. Oregon grape (*Mahonia aquifolium*)

87. Basil (*Ocimum* spp.)

**Mesona.** This is another Javanese species. A decoction of the plant leaves is used to prepare a cooling drink, much consumed locally. Perennial.

**Ceriman.** Found in Mexico and Guatemala. The pulp of the fruits, when strained, makes a delicious drink. Climbing plant.

**Sweet basil.** There are many varieties having different flavours and characteristics. The seeds are the source of a beverage called 'cherbet tokhum', drunk in the Mediterranean lands. Annual.

**Passion-fruit types.** Such species as giant grenadilla, tasco, gullan, and others provide excellent drinks, similar to those produced by Passion fruit.

**Anise plant.** Grows in Europe, Asia and North America. Seeds are used to make anise milk and are the basis of Mediterranean drinks like arak and pastis. Annual.

**Citrange and citrangequat.** Fruits used to

88. Citrange (*Poncirus trifoliata*)

89. Pomegranate (*Punica granatum*)

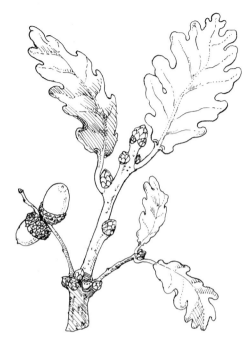

90. European oak (*Quercus robur*)

make squashes and drinks. Several varieties, hybrids of citrus species.

**Plum and cherry substitutes.**   The juices of these fruits may be made into drinks. For different types, see Chapter 7.

**Pomegranate.**   The red or pink pulp is used to make grenadine, a refreshing drink. There are several varieties, such as Wonderful, Selimi, Baghdad, Tunsi, Spanish Ruby, Papershell, Granada Blanca, Jaffa and Galsi, the last named being a white type. Small trees.

**Pear and apple types.**   Juices obtained from these fruits make excellent drinks. For various types, see Chapter 7.

**English or European oak.**   The acorns, after roasting, are used as a substitute for coffee, called *'eichel kaffee'*. Tree.

**Fragrant or sweet-scented sumach.**   Indigenous to eastern North America. The soaked berries are used to make a pleasant and refreshing drink. Shrub.

**Smooth or red sumach.**   Another North American species, of similar habitat to the fragrant sumach. The fruits are made into a cool and pleasant beverage or into a warm, winter drink by mixing with maple sugar. The flowers can also be made into a gargle for treating sore throats. Shrub or small tree.

**Squaw berry, lemonade sumach.**   Found west of the Mississippi and Ohio rivers and in northern Mexico, these fruits can be mashed in water to form a squash or soft drink, of excellent taste.

**Staghorn sumach.**   Also found in eastern North America, this shrub provides acid fruits, which are made into a drink called 'Indian Lemonade'. Shrub.

**Currants.**   Many of these species are made into highly valued soft drinks. They are rich in vitamin C. For different types see Chapter 7.

91. Dog or wild rose (*Rosa canina*)

**Roses.** The ripe fruits of the Californian rose can be made into a pleasant syrup. The leaves of the pomifera and rugosa roses are employed as tea substitutes and also made into beverages, as well as rosewine and rosehoney. The common dog rose, seen in hedges, bears leaves which, when dried, may be used instead of tea.

**Brazilian raspberry.** Fruits are made into soft drinks. Often cultivated.

**European dewberry.** A European shrub. The leaves can be used as a tea substitute.

**Northern dewberry.** A shrub of eastern North America, the fruits of which are made into a syrup, used in pharmaceutical preparations.

**Mora de Castilla.** A raspberry-type plant native to Ecuador. The large fruits are made into a syrup named *'jaropa de mora'*.

**Mora de rocoto, huagra mora.** The fruits are made into a refreshing raspberry-tasting drink. Native to Peru.

**Turkish sage.** Various species of this plant are infused to give a substitute tea in Turkey and Greece. Perennials.

**Thistle sage.** Found in California and Arizona. The seeds are the source of a cooling drink. Perennial.

**Chia.** Indigenous to Mexico. A cool and pleasant-tasting drink is made from the seeds. Perennial.

**California chias.** Two species are used to make popular drinks. Perennials. Natives of western North America.

**Lindenleaf sage.** Native to Mexico and Central America, this plant bears seeds which are used to produce a drink sometimes mixed with barley water. Perennial.

**Sweet broom.** A tropical American shrub. The branches, when placed in drinking water, give it a cool taste and improved flavour.

**Hedge lime, dog lime.** This is a North American species. The seeds are the source of a refreshing drink when mixed with lime juice, claret and syrup. Perennial.

**Imbu, hog plum.** This is a tree which grows in north-east Brazil. The fruits are made into a beverage.

**Samrong.** A tree of south-east Asia. The seeds are made into a refreshing drink in Cambodia.

**Tamarind.** The pods contain a sweet-sour-tasting pulp, which produces good drinks and syrups. The vitamin C content is appreciable, giving the beverage anti-scorbutic properties. Tree, found in the tropics.

**Thelesperma.** Two species of this plant grow in the western parts of the United States. A decoction of the leaves is used to make a pleasant beverage. Annual.

**Grape types.** Various species, such as fox grape, southern fox grape and others provide pleasant-tasting juices for consumption. Vines.

**Cocoas.** Plants of the species *Theobroma* are quite numerous and yield different kinds of cocoas. A list of useful types is given above.

## COCOAS

| Name | Origin |
| --- | --- |
| cacoa montaras or cacao simarron | Colombia |
| Nicaragua cacao tree, cacao blanco or patashti | Mexico and Central America |
| glaucous-leaved cacao | tropical America |
| cacao calabacillo | tropical America |
| herrania mariae | Amazon basin |
| martiana cacao | north Brazil |
| bahia cacao | north Brazil |
| cacao lagarto | Guatemala |
| cacao silvestre or cacao de sonusco | Brazil and Central America |
| cacao de mico (a bitter beverage) | Costa Rico to Panama |
| Guiana cacao | Guiana, Brazil and Peru |

**Tea Substitutes.** A long list of plants (see table below) yield alternatives to ordinary tea, which is produced by the various races of the species *Camellia thea*. The following types can be used in case of necessity. It should be noted that, unless otherwise stated, it is the dried leaves which yield the beverages after infusion with boiling water.

## TEA SUBSTITUTES

| Name | Origin |
| --- | --- |
| hervia, maté, yerba de maté or Paraguay tea | South America |
| khat or cafta | Arabia and Ethiopia |
| Ayapana tea | Brazil, grown in Mauritius and Reunion |
| Jesuit's tea or culen | Chile |
| matara tea | India and Sri Lanka |
| faham or foam tea | Reunion |
| ginnala | Japan and China |
| milfoil or yarrow | temperate zones |
| musk yarrow | central Europe |
| agapetes tea | India |
| iobata tea | Japan |
| marsh mallow | Europe, introduced into the Americas (dried roots used) |
| thé de Bourbon | Reunion |
| aniba tea | Peru |
| aphloia tea | Reunion and Mauritius |
| aplopappus tea | western North America (dried roots used) |
| kutai or caucasian tea | southern Russia |
| southern wood | southern Europe |
| aspalathus tea | Cape Province, South Africa |
| milk vetch | Europe and Siberia |

| | |
|---|---|
| sassafras tea | Tasmania and other southern Australian areas |
| athrixia tea | South Africa |
| bruyère de tonkin | Vietnam (flowers used for tea) |
| borage tea | Mediterranean region (dried flowers used for tea) |
| common heather | Europe and West Siberia |
| catha | Arabia |
| mabi | West Indies (bark used for beverage) |
| thé des canaries | Canary Islands |
| chamaedaphne tea | Northern temperate zone |
| chiogenes tea | Eastern North America |
| chloranthus tea | Java |
| white cistus | Algeria |
| te del monte | Mexico |
| Job's tears | Warm regions. In Japan, parched seeds used for tea |
| American jute | Texas, West Indies, Central America |
| correa or cape barren tea | Tasmania |
| hawthorns | Europe |
| Chaparral tea | south-west United States (flowering tops used as tea) |
| cyclopias | South Africa |
| nardus tea | Java |
| Oldham's desmodium | Japan |
| dithany tea | Siberia |
| malacca tea | Malaysia and Thailand |
| Kaisertee or Schweizertee | subalpine or arctic regions |
| eheretia tea | Philippines |
| longleaf ephedra, desert or teamasters' tea | Mexico and south-western United States |
| kapporie or kapor tea, or iwantschai | Europe, Asia and North America |
| eurya tea | West Indies, Cuba |
| St Helena tea | St Helena |
| kalmuck tea | Siberia and Central Asia |
| hottentot tea | South Africa and Rhodesia |
| amara | Argentina |
| cassena or dahoon holly | east and south-east of North America |
| theezans | Brazil |
| winterberry, black alder or fever bush | eastern North America |
| black drink or yaupon | south and south-east United States |
| Labrador tea | Greenland, Labrador, Canada, northern United States |
| crystal tea ledum | northern hemisphere |
| yellow tea tree | Australia |
| litsea tea | Mexico |

| | |
|---|---|
| moneywort | Europe and North America |
| chamomille tea | Europe and Asia (flowers used as tea) |
| marsh buckbean | Europe, Asia and North America |
| miconia tea | Brazil |
| yerba buena | western North America |
| oswego tea | eastern North America |
| neea tea | Brazil |
| thé des Carolines | east Asia |
| tormentil | Europe, temperate Asia and North America |
| bush cinquefoil | northern hemisphere, especially Alaska |
| cowslip | Europe and temperate Asia |
| Douglas fir, red spruce or red fir | western North America |
| Chilean breadroot | Chile and Peru |
| pennyroyal | Florida |
| pyrola tea | Europe, West Asia, Siberia, Japan and North America |
| Chinese crab apple | China and Assam |
| sageretia or tonkin tea | Burma, Vietnam, India and China |
| broomjute sida | Canary Islands |
| sideritis teas | Greece |
| sweet goldenrod (anise scented tea) | eastern North America |
| rowan tree tea | Europe, West Siberia and Asia Minor |
| teucrium tea | China |
| eastern hemlock | eastern North America |
| little leaf tunic flowers | southern and central Europe, North Africa (dried flowers used for tea) |
| common coltsfoot | Europe, Asia and North America |
| warsaw tea (English elm) | Europe, North Africa, Syria, North Iran, Himalayas and Central China |
| false Paraguay tea, sweet viburnum or nanny berry | eastern North America |
| vitex tea | tropical Africa |
| New Jersey tea or red root | eastern North America |

92. Common coltsfoot (*Tussilago farfara*)

## Alcoholic Drinks

The products, in the form of fruits, seeds or grains, tubers, roots and other portions of large numbers of plants can be made into alcoholic beverages. In particular, the following species are often utilized for this purpose: acacia or mimosa seeds and pods, narasplant, yarrows, coyal, cactus species, albizza, almonds and apricots, cashews, pineapples, custard apples and soursops, strawberry tree, peaches, cereals such as oats, barley, wheat, rice, rye, sorghums, maize, millets, and other grain plants, mahua, coconut, borassus, beets,

93. New Jersey tea (*Ceanothus americanus*)

94. Yarrow (*Achillea millefolium*)

persimmons, berries of different types, figs, cassava, dates, algaroba, apples and pears, plums, sloes, damsons, currants, sugarcane, pepper trees, potatoes, yams, grapes, ginger, jujubes, dandelion, raphia, rhubarb, and numerous other species. In fact, any plant that is edible can probably be made into a liquor.

## Culture of Beverage-yielding Plants

Such a wide range of plants yield beverages that it is not possible to lay down any exact general set of rules regarding their individual special cultures. In practice, these types of lesser-known economic species may be grouped, for growing purposes, under the headings of fruits, leaf crops, and seeds or bulbs, the cultural treatments being adjusted to conform to the needs listed for such classes of plants in previous chapters.

## Preparation of Beverages

Leaves, seeds and roots of plants intended for teas, coffees and cocoas should be dried as soon as possible after harvesting or collection. They are then well crushed or sliced up, in the cases of leaves and roots, or ground into powder if they are seeds. Sometimes roots may be well dried and then milled. The fine powder or the crushed dried leaves should be stored in airtight containers and left to gather aroma and mature.

When preparing soft drinks or squashes, the fruits or other parts of plants should be clean and if necessary carefully washed. They are then cut into pieces, where appropriate, and placed in containers with sugar as required. Boiling water is then poured over the plant material and sugar and the whole well pounded with a wooden spoon, pestle or other implement. Following this, the container should be covered and allowed to cool. When using the mash, dilute to taste and strain through a clean cloth placed over a sieve.

Squashes and soft drinks should be consumed fresh or kept in refrigerators. They cannot be preserved for long periods, unless completely frozen in a freezer. Bottled shop-bought squashes and fruit drinks are treated with chemicals and have no nutritional value.

Instructions for making beers and wines may be found in most good cookery books. These are not difficult to produce at home. Generally the fruit or other plant materials are treated with boiling water, pulped and the mash then strained. The juice resulting from the operations is put into a fermenting vessel and sugar and yeast are added. The fermentation process may take a fortnight to three weeks and during this time the 'must' that rises to the top of the liquor should be skimmed off. When all hissing has ceased, the wine or beer will have formed and should be cleared by adding some isinglass. Bottling can now be carried out. The corks should not be inserted tightly until some two months have elapsed. Different plant materials require individual treatment and beer or winemaking kits can be purchased at chemists' shops, pharmacies or certain large stores, with detailed instructions for use.

To make spirits it is necessary to distil the beer, wine or fermented plant material. This can be done in a still, which will separate the water from the alcohol by a steam process. In some places a licence to operate a home distillery may be required by the local authorities.

## Storing Wines and Beers

Wines of various types are best stored by laying the bottles on their sides, otherwise the corks in the containers may become dry and air can enter. In the case of beers, however, this is unlikely and they may be stored upright. Spirits should be kept upright at all times. Try to keep all liquor in a dark place. Wines, at any rate, and beers as well, do not store well in too-warm conditions, and certainly at temperatures of over 60°F they will deteriorate. In hot areas they can be placed in cellars or deep pits dug in shady spots.

# Chapter 11

# CONDIMENTS

Seasoning herbs or condiments play a vital part in food preparation and they contribute greatly in making our dietary menus more palatable and satisfying. We are all familiar with that common trio of condiments – salt, pepper and mustard – which may be found in practically every home. Indeed, without salt, healthy living would be impossible and its value has always been well understood throughout history. Wars have been fought over salt, revolutions have been born – as when Mahatma Gandhi, the great Indian liberationist, lead the famous 'Salt March' to the sea – and in Roman times soldiers were paid part of their wages in salt, hence the modern word 'salary'. Mustard, too, is very well known and considered essential to proper enjoyment of many meals. As for peppers, without them food would be almost uneatable for those peoples who like hot and spicy dishes, especially in Asia and central or southern American countries.

During the Middle Ages in Europe, when storage facilities for meats were very primitive and flesh for human consumption was often partially rotten, the offensive taste and odour of the food were disguised by the liberal use of condiments and spices, obtained from various plants or herbs, during its preparation and cooking.

Despite these facts, however, we do not today make sufficient use of all the many lesser-known or neglected plants that yield condiments and flavouring or seasoning mat-erials. This is unfortunate because such species not only help to improve the acceptability of foodstuffs, but they also add some nutriment to our daily diet.

The flavour and palatability of food is extremely important. As nutritionists and dieticians know only too well, many excellent foods are rejected by consumers simply because they do not have a familiar or appetizing taste and the flavour may be perhaps unusual. Yet, proper dressing or seasoning with suitable condiments can change the whole picture and render these commodities highly attractive.

## Lesser-known Types of Condiments and Seasoning Herbs

Here are some examples of interesting and useful types:

**Ackawai nutmeg.** A South American tree, found from Guiana to Brazil. It yields fruits that are often substituted for nutmegs.

**Jambolifera.** A species of tropical Asia, the leaves are used as a condiment. Small tree.

**Baobab.** The young leaves are added to soups or to stews to bring out the flavour. Found in Africa, Asia and Australia.

**Aeolanthus.** Native to tropical Africa. Considered to be a herb and employed for flavouring purposes, especially in soups. Perennial.

**Madagascar cardamom.** The seeds are used as a condiment. Indigenous to Madagascar (the Malagasy Republic), the Seychelles and the Mascarene Islands, as well as to East Africa. Perennial.

**Cameroon cardamom.** This plant is the source of a cardamom substitute. Often cultivated. Perennial.

**East African cardamom.** Native to eastern tropical regions of Africa. The seeds supply a condiment. Perennial.

**Grains of paradise.** This plant is found along the Gulf of Guinea. The seeds provide the condiment. Perennial.

**Agastache.** Indigenous to New Mexico. The leaves are used for flavouring dishes. Perennial.

**Galangals.** Species of these plants are found in tropical Asia, especially eastern India, Vietnam, Hainan, Philippine Islands and Java, where the rhizomes are used as condiments. Perennials.

**Ammodaucus.** Zeus's Carrot, a species found in the Sahara oases, the upper Valley of the Nile and Mauritania, produces seeds that are consumed as a condiment in sauces. Perennial.

**Bengal cardamom.** Native to eastern India, often cultivated. Sometimes called the Nepal cardamon. The seeds are dried and ground into a powder employed as a condiment. Perennial.

**Malayan cardamom.** This plant is indigenous to Malaysia. It is frequently cultivated and the seeds are utilized for condimentary purposes, particularly in flavouring cakes. Perennial.

**East Indian cardamom.** Similar to Malayan cardamom.

**Kepulaga cardamom, round cardamom.** This is often cultivated. Perennial. Found in Malaysia.

**Krervanh cardamom.** This plant grows chiefly in the vicinity of Mount Krervanh in Cambodia. It is cultivated and the fruits are used as a condiment. Often added to cordials and sausages. Perennial.

**Java or great cardamom.** Found in the East Indies and Malaysia. Frequently cultivated and used as a condiment. Perennial.

**Nepalese cardamom.** Collected by local farmers in Nepal, this is the source of a condiment. Perennial.

**Krakorso.** A cardamom-type plant, indigenous to south-east Asian countries, especially Indo-China. The fruits are employed as a condiment in various dishes, such as curries. Perennial.

**Bastard Siamese or wild Siamese cardamom.** Native to Burma, but also grown in India and Thailand. Utilized as a condiment. Perennial.

**Androcymbium.** Used by the Tuareg in North Africa as a condiment. Perennial.

**Mugwort.** Found in the northern hemisphere. The young leaves and shoots make a good condiment for goose and pork. Perennial. Mugwort grows about 2–4 feet in height. The leaves are pinnate and the stems ribbed downy with many branches, often purplish in colour. Chinese mugwort is even more aromatic and has longer and darker green leaflets.

**Pichrim bean.** This is a Brazilian tree which bears aromatic seeds used as a condiment.

**Ngai camphor.** Found from Nepal down to Indonesia and the Philippine Islands, this plant has strongly camphor-scented leaves, which are used to flavour food. Shrub.

**Buphthalmum.** The young, aromatic leaves, after drying, are used as a condiment with fish. Indigenous to Vietnam. Shrub.

**Capers.** Besides the well-known caper bush of the Mediterranean region, there are other species which yield similar products. These include aphylla caper, of the Sahara area; corymbifera caper, native to South Africa; Mitchell's caper of Tasmania and Western Australia; and noble caper and dog caper, two other Australian species. (*Illustrated overleaf.*)

**Ajmud.** Found in India and Indo-China. The seeds are used as a condiment. Annual.

**Amboinese coleus.** This plant is used for seasoning meat dishes. It is indigenous to

95. Bush capers (*Capparis spinosa*)

96. Wintersbark (*Drimys winteri*)

Indonesia and Malaysia. Perennial.

**Samphire.**   A plant of the temperate zone, the salty leaves of which form a good condiment. The fruits are egg-shaped and corky, with ridges. They can be used as a substitute for capers or pickled in vinegar. Perennial.

**Zedoary.**   Used as a condiment, often together with, or instead of, the better-known turmeric. The dried rhizomes are ground into powder, which is aromatic and stimulating. Perennial.

**Nardus.**   Found in Indonesia and Sri Lanka (Ceylon), often cultivated, this bears leaves used for condimentary purposes. They are also infused and the resulting liquid drunk as a tea. Perennial grass.

**Fendler's cymopterus.**   A plant of Colorado, Utah and New Mexico in the western United States. The roots are aromatic and, after drying, may be used for flavouring meat dishes. Perennial.

**Cynomorium.**   The roots are dried and ground into a powder which is used as a condiment in North Africa. Shrub.

**Clove bark.**   This is a tree of tropical America. The bark yields clove bark oil, used for flavouring instead of cloves.

**Wintersbark, drimys.**   The bark is ground into powder and used as a condiment in Brazil and Mexico. There is another related species in Australia, the fruits of which may be dried and employed as a substitute for pepper. Trees.

**Eryngium.**   Native of tropical America. The roots have an unpleasant and foetid odour, but when used as a condiment in soups and meat dishes they give a pleasant taste to the food. Perennial.

**Ayapana.**   Found in tropical parts of Asia, this plant is often cultivated. The dried material is used as a condiment. Perennial.

**Wasabi.**   A Japanese species, sometimes cultivated. The ground-up roots are employed as a condiment. Perennial.

**Moroccan ash.**   The fruits are used in the Maghreb in North Africa as a condiment and aphrodisiac. Tree.

**Senegal gynandropsis.**   Indigenous to tropical Africa, India, the Mediterranean and other regions. The ashes of this plant are used as a substitute for salt. Woody species.

**Nigerian or Indian gynandropsis.**   The seeds are anthelmintic and supply an essential oil that has the properties of mustard oil or garlic. Used for flavouring sauces or for stews. Woody plant.

**Tawny day lily.** This species grows in Europe and Asia. The dried leaves are used in China and Japan as a condiment. Perennial.

**Persian heracleum.** A species of Iran. The seeds are utilized as a condiment. Perennial.

**Galanga.** This plant grows in south-east Asia, especially in India, Malaysia and southern Vietnam, where it is cultivated. The rhizome, after drying and grinding into powder, is used as a condiment. Perennial.

**True bay or laurel.** Indigenous to the Mediterranean region, this plant bears seeds that are the source of laurel berry fat or bay fat. The leaves are used as a condiment. Tree.

**Desert pepperweed.** Grows in the south-west United States. The seeds are used for flavouring food. Shrub.

**Lysimachia.** Two species are indigenous to China, Japan, and North Vietnam. The leaves are dried and made into a condiment. Perennial.

**Common balm.** Found in the Mediterranean region, the northern parts of the Middle East, Turkestan and south-western Siberia. It is often cultivated and used for flavouring soups and salads. Perennial.

**Mints.** Field mint is found in temperate areas of Europe, Asia and North America. Bergamot mint has a lemon-like scent and grows in southern Europe, similar regions of Asia and North Africa. American wild mint is indigenous to eastern parts of North America. Perennial herbs. They can be used as substitutes for garden mint.

**Oswego bee balm, oswego tea plant.** The leaves have a mint-like flavour and can be used as a flavouring and condiment. Found in eastern parts of North America. Perennial.

**Lemon bee balm.** This plant grows in New Mexico, Arizona and northern Mexico. It is eaten as a condiment with meat dishes. Perennial.

**Wild bergamot, horse mint, bee balm.** This species is indigenous to North America and is employed as a condiment and dressing with meat. Perennial.

**Pony bee balm.** Native to western North America. It is used for flavouring meat dishes. Perennial.

**Karapincha.** A native of Ceylon, chiefly found in dry areas. The aromatic leaves are used as a condiment, often in curries. Small tree.

**Fenugreek.** The fruits are small and brown, rather like grains. They are aromatic and are employed as a condiment. Frequently cultivated. Annual.

**Horse radish tree.** An Indian tree, acclimatized in many other regions. The leaves and roots are pungent and are said to aid digestion. They can be macerated and mixed with water or milk to form a substitute horse radish sauce to accompany meat dishes.

**Hyssop.** A native of Asia Minor. The leaves may be dried and utilized as a condiment. Aromatic and perennial.

97. Hyssop (*Hyssopus officinalis*)

**Nutmeg substitutes.** Species furnishing products that can be used instead of nutmeg and mace include Macassar or Papua nutmegs, of pungent type; mountain nutmegs of the Indonesian islands of Banda, Amboina and the Moluccas; Bombay, Malabar or wild nutmeg; and Molucca nutmeg. They are all trees.

**Ochocoa.** The seeds are used as a condiment in West Africa. Tree.

**Basil types.** Hoary basil is found in the tropics; Abyssinian basil and holy basil are other species useful for condimentary purposes. Perennials. The Abyssinian basil has been well recommended on account of its flavour, while the hoary basil is said to be good for the skin. Holy or sacred basil is reverenced by Hindus.

**Origanums.** A number of related species may be used instead of the ordinary pot marjoram. A selection is shown below.

ORIGANUMS

| Name | Product | Origin |
|---|---|---|
| Spanish hops | condiment, resembles | southern Europe |
| dictamna hops | thyme in taste | eastern Mediterranean area |
| maghreb hops (two species) | condiments | North Africa |
| onites marjoram | condiment | southern Europe and Asia Minor |

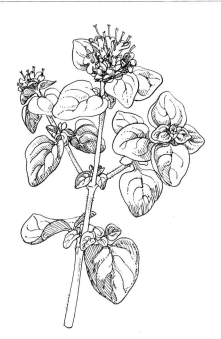

98. Wild marjoram (*Origanum vulgare*)

99. Sweet marjoram (*Origanum majorana*)

**Nzeng.** Found in Gabon, the fruits of this plant are used as a condiment locally.

**Parkia Trees.** The pods and seeds of these trees, of various species, called in Africa 'nittas' or 'locust beans', are used for flavouring and as condiments. Two parkia species grow in Malaysia and the East Indies, the pods having a slight garlic taste.

**Perilla.** The leaves and flower clusters, as well as the cotyledons of young seedlings, are used to make a condiment. Native to China and Japan and also found in India and Korea. Annual. There is also a perennial species, which yields perilla oil.

**Borbonia, red bay, sweet bay.** Indigenous to the south and south-east United States. The dried leaves are used as a condiment, for flavouring soups, and also for crab-gumbo and stuffing roast chicken or other fowls.

**Palmate butterbur, sweet coltsfoot.** This species and a related one grow along the Pacific coastline of North America from British Columbia to California. The ashes from the plants may be used as a source of salt. Perennials.

**Japanese coltsfoot, Japanese petasites.** The slightly bitter flower buds are dried and used as a condiment. Perennial.

**Phaeomeria.** Great phaeomeria is a species native to Malaysia, where it is cultivated. Used for seasoning food. The young flowering shoots are also eaten in curries. Perennial.

**Phellopterus.** Indigenous to Japan and China, as well as to Sakhalin. Often cultivated and used as a condiment. The taste resembles that of tarragon or angelica. Perennial.

**Black carroway.** Found in North Africa, this plant produces seeds which are utilized as a condiment. Perennial.

**Poliomintha.** This species grows in the south-western United States, where the flowers are used for seasoning purposes. Shrub.

**Atlantic mountain mint.** Also termed wild basil, this species is indigenous to the eastern regions of the United States. Perennial.

**Virginian mountain mint.** Another eastern North American plant, the dried buds and flowers of which are used for flavouring meat and soups. Perennial.

**Arabian rue.** Found in Iran, Arabia and North Africa, and used for condimentary purposes. It is moreover the source of an essential oil. Perennial.

**Broom.** A European shrub, which is also naturalized in North America. The leaves and buds are pickled in vinegar and salt and used as capers, called in Germany *'Brahm'* or *'Geiss Kappern'*.

**Niam-niam.** This plant can be seen in countries bordering on the whole Gulf of Guinea, as well as the West Indies. The leaves are used as a condiment in soups. Perennial.

**Marigolds.** The sweet marigold, an annual herb of Mexico and central areas of America, has a tarragon-like flavour and when dried and ground into powder is used as a condiment.

100. Broom (*Sarothamnus scoparius*)

THYMES

| Name | Product | Origin |
|------|---------|--------|
| conehead thyme | dried leaves or oil for flavouring dishes | Mediterranean region, especially Spain |
| Algerian or Saharan thyme | leaves used as condiment | Algeria, Sahara region, Spain |
| Spanish majoram | leaves and oil for flavouring | Mediterranean region |
| creeping thyme | used as condiment and in medicine for coughs | Europe, temperate Asia, Africa and North America |

The pot marigold is a southern European species, the flowers of which are edible and can be dried to produce a condiment for flavouring soups and other dishes. It is said to be very stimulating.

**Thymes.** Besides the garden or common thyme, the species given in the table above provide condiments.

**Guyana unona.** A species found in Guyana. Fruits are used as a condiment. Tree.

**Chinese unona.** Native to tropical Asia. The fruits are employed as a pepper substitute and make a good condiment. The flowers are fragrant. Tree.

**African unona.** Fruits used as a condiment. Tree.

**Zanthoxylum.** Three species of this tree are found in eastern Asia, notably in China, Japan, India, and Indo-China. The seeds or fruits are used as condiments.

**Grains of Selim, Guinea or negro pepper.** This plant is used as a pepper substitute. Often sold in local markets in west Africa, especially in Senegal. Tree.

**Pao d'embira, pimenta de macaco.** A tree, found from Mexico to the Guianas. The fruits have the odour and taste of pepper and are used as a condiment. Several related species provide similar products, including malagueto, frustesca, and silky embira, also of South America; and African pepper.

**Gingers.** The common ginger is produced by the plant *Zingiber officinale*. Some other related types are given in the table below.

GINGERS

| Name | Product | Origin |
|------|---------|--------|
| Amaricans ginger | ginger-tasting rhizomes | Malaysia and Indonesia |
| Cassumunar ginger | ginger-tasting rhizomes used as a condiment | Indo-China |
| Mioga ginger | rhizomes are source of Japanese ginger, which has a bergamot-like flavour. The young flowers, fruits and sprouts are also eaten | Japan |
| Zerumbet ginger | 'Martinique ginger' | grown in Indo-China and West Indies (Martinique) |

101. Ginger (*Zingiber* spp.)

## Culture of Condiments and Seasoning Herbs

The growing of condiments or seasoning herbs is today a very popular pastime. Herbs are best kept together in a small sector of the home garden, because the quantities needed are not large and it is easy to collect them when required or to harvest and dry them for future use in cooking and flavouring food. Where the produce in question consists of leaves, the aim should be to ensure that the plants receive plenty of nitrogen to encourage maximum development of foliage. However, if seeds, fruits or roots are the objective, then ample potash and phosphates will be called for. Always try and keep herb plots free from competing weeds.

## Cooking

After harvesting or collection, the plant material should be properly dried and then crushed, broken up or ground into particles, which are stored in air-tight containers. Only small quantities of condiments are needed to improve the flavour of foodstuffs greatly. Good cooking requires adequate but not excessive seasoning. The amounts to use are listed in cookery manuals, and when any of the above noted substitutes are being employed quantities similar to those of ordinary better-known condiments should be added. It is always best to incorporate minimum amounts at first and as you gain experience with the new condiments, you can increase their usage until you arrive at what you find are the proportions most suited to your own and your family's tastes.

# Chapter 12

# MUSHROOM SUBSTITUTES

The common field mushroom of Europe, *Agaricus campestris*, is considered by many people to be a table delicacy. It is now extensively cultivated under artificial conditions and often sold at very high prices in shops. There are, however, some 250 or more other species of edible mushroom types which are noteworthy and of excellent flavour. All these may be found growing wild in different regions of the world and offer a rich and varied feast to the person who likes this kind of vegetable. Thus there is no actual problem in obtaining substitutes for the cultivated mushroom. Indeed, it is quite simple to collect the wild fungi and grow them in home gardens.

## Nutritional Value

Much has been said and written about the merits and the food value of mushrooms. Some authorities consider that these vegetables are rather overrated as far as their supposed or real contribution to our diet is concerned. Be that as it may, the nutritional content of one cupful (244 grammes) of common mushrooms may be broken down as follows:

| Water | Food energy | Protein | Fat |
|---|---|---|---|
| 93% | 40 Kcal | 5 gm | Trace |

| Carbohydrate | Calcium | Iron |
|---|---|---|
| 6 gm | 15 mg | 1.2 mg |

| VITAMINS | | |
|---|---|---|
| Thiamine | Riboflavin | Niacin |
| 0.4 mg | 0, 60 mg | 4.8 mg |

| Vitamin C | Vitamin A |
|---|---|
| 4 mg | I.U. Trace |

## Avoiding Dangers

Probably more cases of human poisoning have been recorded from fungi than from any other class of plants. It is therefore essential that no one should ever eat any wild mushroom types unless he or she is absolutely certain that the plants in question are safe for consumption and the identification is sure. In cases of any doubt, always refer the specimens first to a botanical authority for checking. To take risks with fungi is highly dangerous. For this reason the botanical names of plant species are given in the list of edible species below to avoid mistakes.

| Name | Location and remarks |
|---|---|
| *Agaricus decastes*<br>*A. luzonicus*, Luzon mushroom<br>*A. Boltoni*, Bolton's mushroom<br>*A. argyrostectus* | Europe, Japan, tropical Asia |

| | |
|---|---|
| *A. manilensis*, Manila mushroom | |
| *A. Merillii*, Merill's mushroom | Europe, Japan, tropical Asia |
| *Amanita caesarea*, Caesar's mushroom | southern Europe; highly esteemed by the Romans |
| *A. ovoidea* | Italy, Portugal, Catalonia and southern France |
| *A. rubescens* | |
| *A. gemmata* | England, Europe and other areas; used in ketchups |
| *A. nivalis* | |
| *A. spissa* | |
| *Armillaria bulbigora* | Sweden |
| *A. matsutake*, matsu take mushroom | Japan |
| *A. mellea* | cosmopolitan; eaten pickled or salted, especially in Austria, Czechoslovakia or eastern Europe |
| *A. ventricosa* | North America and Japan |
| *Auricularia auricula judae*, Jew's ears | temperate zone, especially China, where they are eaten extensively |
| *A. cornea* | |
| *A. tenuis* | |
| *A. brasiliensis*, Brazilian mushroom | tropical areas |
| *A. Moellerii*, Moeller's mushroom | |
| *A. delicata* | Malaysia |
| *Boletus edulis*, Polish mushroom | |
| *B. badius* | |
| *B. appendiculatus* | Europe |
| *B. chrysenteron* | |
| *B. scaber* | |
| *Bovista nigrescens* | |
| *B. plumbea* | North America |
| *B. pila* | |
| *Calvatia cakavu*, kakavu mushroom | |
| *C. umbrinum* | Asia |
| *C. natalense* | |
| *C. cyathiformis*, Omaha mushroom | North America |
| *C. lilacina*, Iroquois mushroom | North America and China |
| *C. gigantea* | |
| *C. candida* | |
| *Cantharellus cibarius*, chanterelle | Europe and other temperate areas |
| *C. cinnabarina* | North America |
| *C. clavatus* | Europe |
| *C. floccosus* | |

| | |
|---|---|
| *C. glutinosus* | Indo-China |
| *Choiromyces Magnusi*, Magnus' mushroom | Southern Europe, especially Sardinia and Portugal |
| *Clavaria aurea*, golden mushroom | Europe |
| *C. Wettsteienii* | |
| *C. flava* | |
| *C. botrytis* | |
| *C. Zippeli*, majang mushroom | Malaysia |
| *Clitocybe hypocalamus* | tropical Asia; grows on calamus or rattan cane species |
| *C. tessulata* | North America; fruitbodies* found on tree branches |
| *Clitopilus prunulus*, mousseron | Europe and Asia |
| *Collybia butyracea* | |
| *C. acerata* | Europe and America, temperate areas |
| *C. distorta* | |
| *C. microcarpa* | tropical Asia, especially Malaysia; fruitbodies found in termite nests |
| *Conchomyces verrucisporus* | |
| *Coprinus ater copel*, copel mushroom | |
| *C. Bryanti* | |
| *C. concolor* | Malaysia |
| *C. confertus* | |
| *C. rimosus* | |
| *C. comatus*, shaggy mane mushroom or shaggy cap | temperate zone; must be eaten soon after picking or will turn black and deteriorate |
| *C. fimetarius* | North America |
| *C. macrorhizus* | tropical Asia, especially Malaysia |
| *C. micaceus* | temperate zone |
| *C. microsporus* | tropical Asia |
| *Cortinarius emodensis*, onglau | |
| *C. ararmillatus* | |
| *C. elatus* | |
| *C. fulgens* | Himalayan regions |
| *C. latus* | |
| *C. multiformis* | |
| *C. violaceus* | |
| *Crepidotus Djamor*, Djamor mushroom | Malaysia and other tropical regions in Asia |
| *Cryptoporus volvatus* | North America and Eastern Asia; fruitbodies grow on wood of conifer trees |
| *Cyttaria Darwinii* *Cyttaria Berteroi* | temperate and subarctic regions of South America; principal vegetable eaten in Patagonia and Tierra del Fuego |
| *Favolus spathulatus* | tropical Asia, especially Sunda Islands |

* The fruitbody is the portion of any mushroom-type plant that is eaten.

*Fistulina hepatica*, vegetable beefsteak, beefsteak fungus, beef tongue, oak tongue or chestnut tongue — temperate zone; fruitbodies are found on tree trunks

*Flamulina velutipes* — temperate zone

*Gomphidius glutinosus* — temperate zone

*G. subroseus*
*G. oregonensis*, Oregon mushroom — western North America

*G. roseus* — Europe and western Siberia

*Gymnopus microcarpus* — Malaysia and Ceylon

*Gyroporus castaneus*
*G. purpurinus*
*G. cyanescens* — temperate and subtropical areas in northern hemisphere

*Helvella crispa*
*H. gigas*
*H. lacunosa*
*H. infulva* — temperate zone

*Hericium coralloides* — temperate and sub-tropical areas

*Hirneola polytricha* — Australia and Asia; a commercial product in China

*Hydnotria carnea*, red truffle — temperate zone; fruitbodies resemble truffles; well liked in Czechoslovakia

*Hydnum fragile* — Java and Malaysia

*Hygrocybe punicea* — temperate zone; red fruitbodies sold in markets in Sweden

*Hygrophorus marzuoles*, marzuole mushroom
*H. chrysodon*
*H. hypothejus*
*H. Queletii*, Quelet's mushroom
*H. lucorum* — Mountain areas in Europe

*H. pratensis* — Europe

*Hypholoma appendiculatum* — temperate zone; fruitbodies may be dried for winter use

*Hyporhodius clypeatus* — Europe and Asia, especially Sweden and parts of Indo-China

*Lactarius congolensis*, Congo mushroom — Zaire

*L. deliciosus*
*L. sanguifluus* — temperate zone, Europe, especially Catalonia, Siberia and Japan

*L. subpurpureus* — North America

*L. helvus*
*L. camphoratus* — Europe; much used after pulverization of fruitbodies in flavouring soups and salads

*L. piperatus* — temperate zone; fruitbodies acrid

*L. torminosus* — temperate zone, especially Sweden and Russia

| | |
|---|---|
| *L. scrobiculatus* ⎫<br>*L. repraesentaneus* ⎬ | temperate zone, especially Russia, where fruitbodies are pickled or salted |
| *L. vellereus* | |
| *L. rufus*, red lactarius mushroom | |
| *L. volemus* | Europe |
| *L. luteolus* | North America |
| *Lacterius hygrophoroides* | eastern Asia and America |
| *L. flavidulus*, imai mushroom | Japan |
| *L. lignyotus* | temperate zone |
| *Lentinus cubensis* | sub-tropical regions |
| *L. edodes*, shiitake mushroom | Japan and China; canned and exported |
| *L. Goossensiae* ⎫<br>*L. lividus*, beeli mushroom ⎬<br>*L. piperatus* ⎭ | Zaire |
| *L. exilis* | Malaya and Philippines |
| *L. sajorcaju*, sajor caju mushroom ⎫<br>*L. connatus* ⎬<br>*L. djamor*, djamor mushroom ⎭ | Malaysia, China, Indo-China, Indonesia and Philippines |
| *L. araucariae* | |
| *L. tuber-regium* | Africa and Malaysia |
| *Lepiota congolensis* | Zaire |
| *L. procerea*, parasol mushroom ⎫<br>*L. mastoides* ⎬<br>*L. rachodes* ⎭ | temperate zone |
| *Lycoperdon perlatum*, puffball mushroom ⎫<br>*L. fuligineum* ⎪<br>*L. piriforme* ⎬<br>*L. pratense* ⎪<br>*L. umbrinum* ⎭ | tropical Asia |
| *L. gemmatum* | North America and other temperate regions |
| *Morchella esculenta*, common morel and other *Morchella* species | cosmopolitan |
| *Panus rudis* | cosmopolitan; fruitbodies used in Georgia (Caucasus) in the preparation of a sheep's milk cheese called *'airan'* |
| *Pholiota cylindrica* | Mediterranean region |
| *P. marginata* | North America |
| *P. nameko*, nameko mushroom ⎫<br>*P. terrestris* ⎬<br>*P. squarrosoides* ⎭ | Japan |
| *P. squanosa* | North America |
| *Pleurotus anas* ⎫<br>*P. fissilis* ⎬ | Indonesia |
| *P. eryngii*, cardarellas mushroom | Italy |

| | |
|---|---|
| *P. ostreatus*, oyster mushroom | cosmopolitan; eaten in China, eastern USSR and Germany |
| *Pluteus cervinus* | cosmopolitan |
| *Podaxis pistillaris* | Africa and Australia |
| *Polyporus arcularius* | Malaysia |
| *P. Farlowii*, Farlow's mushroom | south-western United States; may be stored for winter use |
| *P. frondosus* | temperate zone |
| *P. grammocephalus* | tropical Asia |
| *P. udus* | Java |
| *P. vibecinus* | Pacific islands |
| *P. ovinus* <br> *P. Pes Caprae* <br> *P. cristata* <br> *P. squamosus* | temperate zone |
| *P. sulfureus* | cosmopolitan |
| *P. tuckahoe*, tuckahoe mushroom | north-western North America |
| *P. tunetanus* | Mediterranean region |
| *P. versipellis* | temperate zone; pickled and known as 'krassny grib' in Russia |
| *Pompholyx sapidum* | central and eastern Europe |
| *Poria cocos*, Indian or tuckahoe bread | temperate zone; grows on tree roots |
| *Psalliota arvensis*, field mushroom | temperate zone |
| *Rajapa eurhiza*, djamoeur rajap | tropical Asia; grows in termite nests |
| *Rhizopogon rubescens* | Japan; fruitbodies grow subterraneously |
| *Rhodopaxillus amethystinus* | Indonesia |
| *R. nudus* | Europe and Japan; sometimes cultivated on dead leaves in cellars, especially in France |
| *R. caffrorum* | South Africa |
| *Rozites caperata* <br> *Russula alutacea* | Europe |
| *R. mariae* <br> *R. vesca* <br> *R. virescens* <br> *R. flava* | Europe |
| *R. atrovirens* | Zaire |
| *Sparassis crispa* <br> *S. laminosa* | temperate zone |
| *Terfezia Boudieri* | North Africa and Asia Minor |
| *Tirmania africana*, African mushroom | North Africa; normally collected late in October |
| *Tremella fuciformis* | tropics and sub-tropics; eaten largely in China |

| | |
|---|---|
| *Tricholoma equestre* | |
| *T. pessundatum* | |
| *T. columbetta* | Europe and Japan |
| *T. flavobrunneum* | |
| *T. georgii*, George's mushroom | Europe |
| *T. mongolica*, Mongolian mushroom or paikumo | Mongolia, Manchuria and China |
| *T. rutinlans* | temperate zone |
| *Tuber aestivum*, truffle | Europe, chiefly Mediterranean region; important commercial commodity, collected in summer and late autumn, using trained dogs to smell out the subterranean fungi |
| *T. brumale*, truffe violette | central and southern Europe, especially northern Italy, France, Switzerland and southern Germany |
| *T. excavatum*, truffe jaune | central Europe, northern Italy, France and England |
| *T. gennadii*, quiza or tartufi bianchi | Mediterranean region and Canary Islands |
| *T. magnatum*, truffe grise or truffe blonde | northern Italy and France |
| *T. melanospermum*, truffe de France, truffe franche or truffe vraie | northern Italy, Spain and France |
| *T. unicinatum*, truffe de la Bourgogne | central and southern Europe |

## Culture of Mushroom Substitutes

Where it is desired to grow edible fungi at home or in the garden, the normal procedures used for ordinary mushrooms will serve best. This means providing beds of horse manure (often very difficult to obtain these days in many countries) or prepared compost, and shelter from climatic extremes. Here is a simple and easy way of making a growing medium at home for edible fungi crops.

Take 300 lbs of straw, place it on a large polyethylene sheet, a tarpaulin, or on concrete, and wet it thoroughly with water. Leave this for two days. Then mix together 100 lbs of sawdust, 30 lbs of bran or flaked oatmeal (porridge oats), and enough water to moisten them. Add 9 lbs of ammonium sulphate, 9 lbs of superphosphate, and 4 lbs of urea fertilizer. Make sure that all the nutrient salts are absorbed and the whole lot is well mixed. Now combine the straw with the sawdust, bran or oats and fertilizers and pile the entire mixture into a heap about 4 feet long by 3 feet wide by some 3 feet high. Water well so that the material is quite wet, with some seepage from the bottom of the heap.

In two days, the temperature of the heap should rise to 140–160°F. On the sixth day, turn the material for the first time, by removing one foot of the compost from the sides and top of the heap, breaking up the remainder, and replacing so that the outer parts now form the inside and the inner portions become the outside. This procedure allows gas exchange to occur. While turning, sprinkle 10 lbs of calcium carbonate over the material. Apply more water, ensuring that no dry patches are left in the heap. The temperature will rise again to about 150°F. On the tenth day, turn for the second time, and then on the thirteenth day give a further turn, sprinkling $12\frac{1}{2}$ lbs of gypsum powder (calcium sulphate) over the material. Reform the heap, as before, and make additional turns on the sixteenth and the nineteenth days. On the twentieth day, break down the heap, spreading it out on the polyethylene sheet or concrete base and sprinkling $\frac{1}{2}$ lb of Lindane insecticide over the compost to check any pests that may be present. The material should be dark brown in colour, without any objectionable odour, and possessing ample moisture when pressed in the palm of the hand. This is the medium for growing mushroom substitutes. It can be placed in beds or boxes and pressed down gently, the spawn of the fungi being inserted into it. If necessary, after putting the compost into the beds or boxes, spray it carefully with a little water to increase the natural humidity. The temperature should then rise to about 138–140°F. Maintain this heat for two days, then allow it to fall to 75°F by extra ventilation. It is now ready for planting.

## Cooking

There are numerous ways of cooking and eating mushroom-type vegetables. For example, they can be made into omelettes, patties, soups, puddings, salads, sauces, soufflés and stuffing, or may be consumed fried, baked in butter or wines, grilled or with cheese. Often they are bottled or quick-frozen for keeping in the home freezer. Details of the various dishes and recipes for them will be found in cookery books, as well as instructions on preserving for later usage.

# Chapter 13

# CUCURBITS, GOURDS AND MELONS

Generally speaking, the cucurbits, which include gourds and melons, as well as pumpkins, squashes and marrows, fall within the category of climbers and are often annuals. They are excellent as vegetables. Common examples that we may see growing in gardens or offered for sale in shops are cucumbers, marrows and ordinary melons. These kinds of plants are frequently monoecious – that is to say, they have the sexes in separate flowers on the same plant, but in some cases they may be dioecious, with the sexes on separate plants. They grow quite rapidly and need fairly rich, friable soils and abundant moisture around the roots. However, waterlogging of the ground is a serious impediment to good development. A reasonably dry climate or not-too-humid conditions in a greenhouse are best. Irrigation is necessary in hot periods, because excessive dryness will cause rapid wilting of the plants. Mature gourds are remarkable for their keeping qualities. After harvesting, in some instances, they will store well for months.

We can divide this range of vegetables and fruits into seven main sections: cucumbers, melons and water melons, gourds, pumpkins, squashes, marrows, and various other types. Inevitably many plants overlap these classes, which are not of course scientific divisions but merely popular classifications. Nevertheless, they serve to remind us of the purposes which each group has and the ways in which we can use them in our diets. There are numerous species of useful and palatable lesser-known plants in these categories which can be employed as good substitutes for the ordinary cucumbers, marrows and melons or other household vegetables and fruits. A selection of different kinds suitable for contrasting climatic conditions has been listed, but it should be remembered that tropical and sub-tropical species can always be grown without difficulty under glass in cold countries.

## Cucumbers

**Mandera or Zanzibar cucumber.** A native of East Africa. The fruits are often pickled. Annual.

**Anguria, West Indian gherkin, gooseberry gourd.** This plant bears small cucumber-like fruits, which are generally eaten boiled or made into pickles. Annual.

**Oriental pickling melon.** Indigenous to China and Japan. Very young fruits are used in soups and mature ones made into pickles. Annual.

**Metuliferus cucumber.** Found in tropical Africa. Often cultivated and used in salads.

**Trigone cucumber.** An Australian species, consumed locally. Perennial.

**Melocoton, casabanana.** A species of tropical America, bearing stout cucumber-like fruits, about 10–15 inches long and 3 inches wide. They are eaten when green. Perennial vine.

## Melons and Water Melons

There are a number of types of melons or muskmelons, also called canteloupes. The popular varieties are divided into groups, including those called Jenny Lind, Netted Gem, Pollock, Hackensack, Tip Top, Osage, Hoodoo, Burell's Gem, and Persian. Subdivisions range from reticulates to netted and nutmeg melons, European canteloupes, pineapple melons, winter honeydew, casaba, orange melon (utilized for preserves), pomegranate melons, Queen Anne's pocket melon, and Oriental pickling melons. Some of these are not well known to the public.

**Watermelon.**   Here also we have numerous varieties, such as Florida Favourite, Black Diamond, Klondyke, Tom Watson, Angelo, New Hampshire Midget, and Stone Mountain. The citron watermelon is used in pickles and preserved in syrup. There are two good varieties: Red Citron and Green Giant.

## Gourds

**Ash punpkin, white gourd, Wax gourd.** This plant grows in warm areas or under glass in temperate zones. The large ovoid fruit is covered with a whitish waxen bloom. It is used as a vegetable. Annual.

**Bottle gourd, calabash gourd.** Suited chiefly to semi-dry districts, the fruits are 16–24 inches in length and resemble a large decanter. The plant is an annual and has white flowers. The gourds are boiled and eaten as a vegetable, but when fully ripe the shell hardens and they can be employed as vessels for water or other liquids.

**Dishcloth gourd.**   About 8–10 inches long with prominent sharp ridges. Often used as a curry vegetable, the outer skin being peeled off before cooking. Annual.

**Snake gourd.**   Bears long, cylindrical and green or greenish-white fruits, 4–6 feet in length. It is sliced and boiled for culinary purposes. Annual.

**Sinkwa towel gourd.**   This plant furnishes fruits 8–10 inches long with sharp ridges. When tender they make excellent vegetables. Annual.

**Loofah.**   The cylindrical fruits are 8–14 inches in length. When young and tender they can be eaten as vegetables; when mature they are fibrous and form the loofahs of commerce, sold for scouring the body while bathing. Annual.

**Tumpai.**   A small, oblong, warty-looking gourd much eaten as a vegetable in tropical parts of Asia. The shoots and leaves are also edible. Annual.

**Moschata.**   A large ovoid or round gourd, with yellow spots and dark green patches or streaks. Annual.

**Bitter gourd, charantia, karela.**   Yields bitter fruits, excellent for pickling or use in curries. The gourds are 6–8 inches in length and yellow to bright orange in colour when ripe. There are several varieties. Annuals.

**Wild gourd.**   The seeds are used as food in the south west of the United States and adjacent districts of Mexico. Perennial.

## Pumpkins

The pumpkins belong to the species *Cucurbita maxima*, and vegetable marrows to that called *Cucurbita pepo*. There are numerous varieties of different sizes, shapes and colours.

## Squashes

These are called botanically *Cucurbita melopepo*. There are numerous varieties and strains of different types and colours, ranging from ovoid to almost flat or shell-like forms. They prefer drier districts. Annuals.

## Other Cucurbits

**Ficifolia.**   Found in eastern Asia. Often cultivated. The fruits are eaten boiled and may be preserved. Perennial.

**Coccinea.** Fruits are eaten raw, cooked or candied. The shoots are also edible. Perennial.

**Pepino de Comer.** Native to Peru and Bolivia. The fruits are used as a vegetable and also made into pickles. Annual.

**Achocha.** Another South American species. The fruits are consumed as a vegetable. Annual.

**Elaterium.** Found in Central America. The young fruits are edible and are used as a vegetable after cooking. Perennial.

**Tacaco.** Indigenous to Costa Rica. The fruits are boiled and eaten locally. Often cultivated. Perennial.

**Curuba or casa banaya.** The fruits are consumed as a vegetable or made into preserves. A South American species, well liked in Peru and Brazil. Perennial.

**Cucumber gourd.** A species of tropical parts of Asia and Northern Australia. Fruits eaten locally. Well liked by Hindus. Annual.

**Japanese gourd.** Native to Japan, often cultivated. The young fruits are salted or kept in soya sauce for eating. Perennial.

## Culture of Cucurbits

Cucumber types and related species grow most vigorously with a good level of humidity, but with the proviso that if the atmospheric moisture is excessive there is a danger of mildew and rotting of fruit stems. There should be no checks in development and the plants must always have enough water or they will wilt rapidly. A good general level of nutrition is important to secure the best produce, with balanced quantities of nitrogen, potash, phosphates and calcium. This can be secured with well-made compost, supplemented by light dressings of ammonium sulphate, potash salts, superphosphate and calcium nitrate, at a total of not over one ounce to each square yard of garden space weekly. The fertilizer salts should not be allowed to fall on the leaves of plants, since this could cause burning. In hot areas, shading is desirable, and in cold localities, heat will be required in winter months. Waterlogging of the soil should be avoided. Supports are needed to enable the plants to climb.

## Cooking

Cucumbers are generally eaten raw, sliced, and incorporated into salads. They also make excellent sandwiches. Marrows, pumpkins and squashes can be cooked by boiling and consumed as an ordinary vegetable, or else fried, mashed, used for soups, stuffed, dressed with cheese, or prepared in a variety of ways. Pumpkin pie is also very popular. Recipes will be found in cookery books. Pumpkins store well and can be kept for several months after harvesting.

# Chapter 14

# MISCELLANEOUS PLANTS

Various kinds of plants, little-known to most people, produce useful products that can serve well in times of shortage or scarcity or as cheaper and more natural alternatives to many common items of daily food. Here are a few suggestions for the attention and consideration of readers in different areas.

## Sugar Substitutes

When sugar is unavailable or too costly, the following plants can provide sweetening:

**Indian sugar tree.** This species grows in northern India. It is called botanically *Madhuca latifolia*. The flowers are rich in nectar and are a good source of sugar, used for sweetening food as well as for fermented liquors and acetone. It has been recommended for commercial purposes.

**Sweet mastic, sweet African olive.** The fresh, ripe fruits of this tree, native to tropical Africa, have the property of imparting a sweet taste to anything that is bitter, acid or sour, if it is eaten immediately.

**Sweet millet.** This grass is found in Central Africa and the Sudan. It supplies a sweet and thick syrup, which is used in confectionary. Perennial.

**Sweet hemp.** This is found in South America, especially Paraguay. The plant contains estevin, a glucosid which is one hundred and fifty times sweeter than sugar. A good sweetening agent. Perennial.

## Confectionary Plants

Many plant products are used in confections. Some are well-known, such as those mixed into chocolates, toffees and cakes commonly sold to the public. But there are others, less often used, which can add greatly to the flavour, as well as to the food value, of candies, sweets and other confections. Some interesting items are listed in the table below.

| CONFECTIONARY PLANTS | |
|---|---|
| *Name* | *Product* |
| sugar, silver or white maple (trees)* | sources of maple sugar |
| calamus, sweet flag or flag root (perennial) | rhizomes candied |
| camel's thorn (shrub) | sugary exudation used as a sweetmeat found in Middle East |
| cherry gum (tree) | source of cherry gum, Persian gum or kirschgummi, consumed in Iran and Arabia |

* Illustrated on page 153.

| | |
|---|---|
| almondette tree | seeds sold under name of almondettes; native to India and Malaysia |
| pilinut (tree) | seeds when roasted have good flavour and are used for confections; found in Philippines |
| craniolaria (annual) | fleshy roots are preserved in sugar and considered a delicacy in West Indies |
| echinocactus (cactus) | pulp used for making sweets; found in south-western parts of United States |
| eletaria or Java cardamon (perennial) | fruits are candied |
| Wislizen's cactus | pulp of stems made into candy sold in USA and Mexico |
| papaya orejona (tree) | fruits made into sweetmeats in Mexico |
| garden lovage (perennial) | fruits used for flavouring sweets; found in Europe |
| lotos (water plant) | rhizomes preserved in sugar as confection; eastern Asiatic species |
| opuntias (cacti) | found in south-western North America and Central America; the different sweetmeats prepared from the fruits include *miel de tuna, melcoacha* and *coloncha* |
| European turkey oak (tree) | a white substance called 'oak manna', *'gaz'* or *'gazu'* is produced by this tree and used for making a sweet called *'gazenjubeen'* |
| eglantine rose (shrub) | flowers are source of *gulangabin*, used in confections and composed of rose petals and honey |
| telosma (climber) | fleshy roots made into sweetmeat popular in Java |
| Japanese torreya (tree) | kernels of nuts used in Japan for confections; highly esteemed |
| trapa (water plant) | seeds preserved in honey and sugar in China, Korea and Japan |
| vanillas (vines) | apart from the official vanilla there are substitutes: vanilla of Bahia or Brazil, Guayana vanilla, West Indian or Phaeantha vanilla, and pompona bova or vanilla bouffie; these are all beans |
| jujubes (shrubs) | fruits made into glacé fruit or preserved in honey and sugar; several species found in warm dry areas |

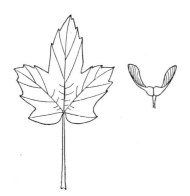

102. Sugar maple (*Acer saccharum*)

103. Cactus (*Opuntia* var.)

104. European Turkey oak (*Quercus cerris*)

## Other Useful Varieties

**Screwpine.**   This species grows in warm regions of Asia. The fruits are soft and sweet, with a pleasant, pineapple-like taste. Much eaten locally.

**High vitamin C content or anti-scorbutic types.**   A woody plant called gynandropsis, quite common in the tropics, especially in Nigeria and India, produces leaves used for flavouring, with a high vitamin C value. Another species specially rich in this vitamin is spoonwort, scorbute grass or scurvy grass, found in Europe and temperate regions of Asia. Wintersbark (drimys), a tree native to South America and Mexico, has similar properties, the bark being employed for supplying ascorbic acid.

**Gamote.**   Native to western North America, especially Kansas. The young roots are a good substitute for parsnips and have similar values.

**Opium substitute.**   Griffith's fraxinus or Himalayan ash is a good substitute for opium and can help in treatment of addiction: the leaves can be smoked and produce the same scent and taste as opium, but do not possess its narcotic properties or induce the unpleasant effects of that drug.

**Horse chestnut.**   The seeds may be used for making a good meal if the tannin and a glucosid are first removed. Horse chestnut flour has been employed for baking bread. Apart from the ordinary horse chestnut, there are also the California buckeye and the red buckeye, which yield seeds suitable for the same purpose. The seeds are usually prepared for milling into flour by boiling or maceration.

105. Horse chestnut (*Aesculus hippocastanum*)

**Amanita, fly mushroom.** Native to the temperate regions, the fruitbodies can be boiled in water with added sugar to produce a decoction for killing flies. This is very important in removing one of the main causes of food spoilation.

**Algae.** Numerous kinds of algae are used for food and food preparation. These include types of the blue-green, green, red, and brown algae. The families and species are too extensive to list here in detail and may require fairly skilled recognition, so it is best to consult local institutions to advise on edible types in particular districts. Some common species are given below.

**Murlins, bladder locks.** Brown algae, the 'fingers' and sweet midribs of which are used as food in some parts of Scotland and Ireland.

**Ecklonia.** About six species of these plants are eaten in Japan and China.

**Undaria.** Found on the eastern coasts of Asia and eaten in China and Japan, when roasted or boiled in vinegar.

**Dictyota and dictyopteris.** These algae are indigenous to the Pacific region. Notable amongst them are Hawaiian sea weed limu lipoa.

**Bull kelp.** Eaten in Australia and New Zealand as a food; also used in southern Chile for making into soups and as a vegetable.

**Bladder wrack, lady wrack, sea ware, black tang, bladder fucus.** Found in the North Atlantic region and has a good vitamin C content. Also used for goitre and treatment of obesity, as well as winter feed for livestock.

**Horsetail kelp, seaweed, tangle, sea girdles, sea-staff.** Used for food when young and also in the manufacture of algin, an ingredient of processed foods, ice creams, jellies, pharmaceutical commodities, cosmetics and lotions. It also has industrial applications. A North Atlantic species.

**Japanese kelp.** Native to eastern parts of the Asian coastline. It is the source of *kombu* in Japan which is used in many food dishes and for confections. Also employed as a substitute for tea, and in China it is eaten with pork. There are several similar related species.

**Australian sea weed.** Eaten in Australia.

**Sweet tangle, broadleaf kelp.** A North Atlantic type, which is used for making into algin.

Other useful species are: cladosiphon or okam, mesogloia, the phyllitis or awa and sagami seaweeds of Japan, as well as several more of comparable type.

There are two main families of blue-green algae, five of green and sixteen of red algae. Very many of the plants belonging to these groups have economic importance for food supplies. For readers interested in sampling or utilizing such forms of nutriment, reference lists may be consulted in books on the flora of different countries, available locally, or in works on economic botany. Aid in identification may be sought from the nearest herbarium or botanical institution.

## Culture

The artificial cultivation of the types of algae listed above has been undertaken successfully using plastic tubes and a hydroponic solution. Details may be found in books on hydroponics or on algae culture.* The produce, after drying, is made into edible cakes or flavoured and processed into meat and vegetable substitutes.

The various other plants mentioned in this chapter cover a wide range of lesser-known food types, and when growing them reference should be made to the notes already given in the chapters on fruits, roots and seeds.

* See *Advanced Guide to Hydroponics*, chapters 10 and 21 (Pelham Books, 1976).

*Appendices*
*Index*

# Appendix I:

# AVERAGE NUTRITIONAL VALUES OF SOME PLANTS (per 100 grammes)

| item | protein % | fat % | calcium mg | iron mg | vitamin A IU | thiamine (vitamin B₁) mg | riboflavin mg | niacin mg | vitamin C (ascorbic acid) mg |
|---|---|---|---|---|---|---|---|---|---|
| amaranth leaves | 2·4 | ·5 | 177 | 2·8 | 6100 | ·04 | ·16 | ·9 | 61 |
| dandelion | 2·4 | ·6 | 135 | 2·8 | 9000 | ·17 | ·13 | ·7 | 25 |
| chavote | ·8 | ·2 | 9 | ·5 | 30 | ·02 | ·03 | ·3 | 12 |
| good King Henry | 2·3 | ·3 | 70 | 2·7 | 8000 | ·08 | ·16 | ·5 | 50 |
| comfrey | 2·0 | ·5 | 200 | 2·9 | 5500 | 0·5 | ·12 | ·7 | 55 |
| alfalfa* or lucerne | 4·2 | 2·1 | 175 | 2·5 | 6500 | 0·4 | ·15 | ·8 | 60 |
| kankun and sweet potato leaves (*Ipomoea* spp.) | 2·4 | ·3 | 80 | 2·5 | 5850 | ·09 | ·14 | ·6 | 36 |
| vine and country spin-aches | 1·8 | ·2 | 68 | 2·4 | 7700 | ·09 | ·16 | ·5 | 50 |
| Indian and Japanese mustards | 1·8 | ·2 | 157 | 2·5 | 4700 | ·07 | ·17 | ·6 | 85 |
| field beans† | 22·5 | 1·7 | 137 | 6·7 | 30 | ·54 | ·18 | 2·1 | 3 |
| lablab beans | 22·5 | 1·5 | 92 | 4·6 | 250 | ·63 | ·16 | 1·6 | 1 |
| sword beans | 23·5 | 3·9 | 141 | 7·4 | 30 | ·56 | ·11 | 1·1 | 1 |
| lima beans | 19·7 | 1·1 | 85 | 5·2 | 30 | ·46 | ·16 | 1·8 | 1 |
| mung beans | 23·0 | 1·3 | 145 | 7·8 | 300 | ·56 | ·17 | 2·0 | 5 |
| cluster beans | 29·5 | 1·4 | 105 | 6·5 | 200 | ·55 | ·12 | 1·7 | 2 |
| lentils | 24·5 | 1·9 | 56 | 6·1 | 100 | ·50 | ·21 | 1·8 | 3 |
| moth beans | 23·8 | 0·7 | 160 | 7·0 | 250 | ·50 | ·13 | 1·5 | 2 |
| peas | 22·5 | 1·8 | 65 | 4·8 | 100. | ·72 | ·15 | 2·4 | 4 |
| pigeon peas | 22·5 | 1·7 | 130 | 5·8 | 130 | ·50 | ·14 | 2·3 | 4 |
| chick peas | 24·5 | 4·5 | 149 | 7·2 | 300 | ·40 | ·18 | 1·6 | 5 |
| cow peas | 24·0 | 1·8 | 76 | 5·7 | 40 | ·92 | ·18 | 1·9 | 2 |
| vetching | 31·9 | 0·9 | 100 | 4·9 | 300 | ·76 | ·19 | 1·7 | 2 |
| horse gram | 22·5 | 1·7 | 91 | 4·6 | 250 | ·62 | ·16 | 1·6 | 1 |
| Job's tears | 13·8 | 5·1 | 21 | 3·6 | — | ·28 | ·19 | 4·3 | — |
| buckwheat | 11·0 | 2·0 | 30 | 3·2 | — | ·24 | ·15 | 2·9 | — |
| quinoa | 19·0 | 5·0 | 119 | 7·3 | — | ·33 | ·21 | 1·6 | — |
| ragi | 6·5 | 1·7 | 350 | 4·0 | 100 | ·35 | ·05 | 1·5 | — |
| proso | 11·8 | 2·4 | 30 | 4·0 | — | ·78 | ·10 | 1·0 | — |
| pearl millet | 11·7 | 4·7 | 28 | 4·0 | 200 | ·33 | ·15 | 2·1 | — |
| little millet | 10·2 | 3·0 | 30 | 4·0 | — | ·30 | ·10 | 1·0 | — |
| cockspur | 12·0 | 3·0 | 40 | 4·0 | — | ·30 | ·15 | 1·5 | — |

| item | protein % | fat % | calcium mg | iron mg | vitamin A IU | thiamine (vitamin B$_1$) mg | riboflavin mg | niacin mg | vitamin C (ascorbic acid) mg |
|---|---|---|---|---|---|---|---|---|---|
| koda | 11·7 | 2·1 | 35 | 4·0 | — | ·30 | ·10 | 2·0 | — |
| bulrush | 11·3 | 3·3 | 40 | 4·0 | — | ·30 | ·12 | 2·0 | — |
| *Ipomoea* spp. (tubers and roots) | 1·0 | ·4 | 29 | ·9 | 425 | ·08 | ·05 | ·5 | 20 |
| *Xanthosoma* spp. (yautia, etc) | 1·7 | ·3 | 11 | ·9 | negligible | ·07 | ·03 | ·5 | 9 |
| arracacha | 1·3 | ·2 | 15 | ·6 | 220 | ·05 | ·04 | 1·5 | 20 |
| giant taro | 1·6 | ·2 | 20 | ·9 | negligible | ·12 | ·02 | ·8 | 5 |
| oca | 1·9 | ·7 | 5 | 1·1 | 40 | 0·5 | ·04 | ·7 | 35 |
| salsify | 2·5 | ·5 | 31 | 1·2 | 10 | ·03 | ·04 | ·2 | 10 |
| Chinese chive | ·8 | ·1 | 39 | ·5 | 20 | ·03 | ·02 | ·2 | 9 |
| Heracleum lanatum | ·9 | ·2 | 35 | ·6 | 10 | ·05 | ·04 | ·8 | 30 |
| chayote roots | 1·0 | ·3 | 10 | ·5 | 35 | ·02 | ·03 | ·4 | 14 |

* Alfalfa seeds, sprouted and harvested at 5–7 days' growth, for use in salads, contain up to 40% protein and increased vitamins.

† Note: Compare the items in the list from field beans to horse gram with beef (14% protein); pork (10·5% protein); poultry (12% protein); fresh fish (about 10–18%); and lobsters (6·6% protein).

*Sources:* Food and Agriculture Organization of the United Nations; Government of India; author's researches

# Appendix II:

# SOURCES OF SEEDS AND PLANT MATERIAL

Some comments on obtaining stocks of seeds of lesser-known food plants may be found in the preface to this book.

If you are unable to obtain supplies locally, the procedure is as follows. Look up the country or countries situated in the areas where the plant in question grows (you can see its natural habitat listed in this book after the name of the plant) and write to the Director, Ministry or Department of Agriculture, in the *capital city* of the country concerned. Sometimes, of course, there may be only one country in which to enquire, but often there may be several. Ask for a supply of seed to be sent to your address. Normally, most government agricultural departments are only too happy to help, and they may give you names of seedsmen or growers in their areas. A specimen enquiry letter is given below.

Other sources of information are Food and Agriculture Organization of the United Nations, Rome, Italy; United States Department of Agriculture, Beltsville, Maryland, USA; Ministry of Agriculture, Fisheries and Food, Whitehall, London SW1, UK; and Royal Botanic Gardens, Kew, Surrey, UK.

In case of difficulty, the author will be glad to give advice. Letters should be addressed to him care of Pelham Books Ltd., 52 Bedford Square, London WC1, UK.

## Commercial Suppliers

Thompson and Morgan Ltd.,
London Road,
Ipswich, Suffolk,
IP2 OBA,
UK.

Vilmorin-Andrieux et Cie.,
4 Quai de Mégisserie,
75001 Paris,
France.

*(This firm can obtain most kinds of seeds through their local agents in all parts of the world)*

## Specimen Enquiry Letter

*From:*  name..................................................................................................................

   address ............................................................................................................

   .......................................................................................................................

   .......................................................................................................................

*To:*  The Director
   Ministry or Department of Agriculture
   city...................................................................................................................
   country..............................................................................................................
   date : ..............................................................................................................

Reference :
[enter name(s) of plant(s) required*]

I am writing to ask if you would be kind enough to supply me with . . . [quantity] seeds or planting material of the above noted plant(s) which I understand grow(s) in your country. I am very anxious to cultivate the species in my farm/garden/plantation, so your help will be much appreciated.

Alternatively, can you give me the names of commercial suppliers or growers who could assist me?

Please send a phytosanitary certificate when despatching the seeds, and advise me of any costs involved.

Many thanks for your help.

Yours sincerely,

[signature]

* Always use botanical or Latin names of species. (See index.)

# FURTHER READING

Bailey's *Cyclopedia of American Agriculture* and *Standard Cyclopedia of Horticulture*, recent editions (New York)

Hill, A. F., *Economic Plants* (Van Nostrand, New York)

Lange, M., and Hora, F. B., *guide to Mushrooms and Toadstools* (W. Collins Sons & Co., Ltd., London)

Macmillan, H. F., *Tropical Planting and Gardening* (Macmillan & Co., Ltd., London)

McClintock, D., and Fitter, R. S. R., *Guide to Wild Flowers* (W. Collins Sons & Co., Ltd., London)

Uphof, J. C. T., and Englemann, H. R., *Dictionary of Economic Plants* (Weinheim, Germany)

*Flora.* Practically every country today publishes its own flora, which will be found locally. The issuing authority will normally be the Botanical Survey Department of the country in question.

The journal *Economic Botany* (New York, Published since 1947) is also useful.

# INDEX

*The popular names of plants are given, followed by their Latin or botanical equivalents*